Albert Einstein

And the Frontiers of Physics

Owen Gingerich
General Editor

Albert Einstein

And the Frontiers of Physics

Jeremy Bernstein

Oxford University Press
New York • Oxford

Oxford University Press

Oxford New York
Athens Auckland Bangkok Bogotá Bombay
Buenos Aires Calcutta Cape Town Dar es Salaam
Delhi Florence Hong Kong Istanbul Karachi
Kuala Lumpur Madras Madrid Melbourne
Mexico City Nairobi Paris Singapore
Taipei Tokyo Toronto
and associated companies in
Berlin Ibadan

Design: Design Oasis
Layout: Leonard Levitsky
Picture research: Lisa Kirchner

Library of Congress Cataloging-in-Publication Data
Bernstein, Jeremy
Albert Einstein
p.   cm. — (Oxford portraits in science)
Includes bibliographical references and index.
ISBN 0-19-509275-9
1. Einstein, Albert, 1879-1955—Biography—Juvenile literature.
2. Physicists—Biography—Juvenile literature.
[1. Einstein, Albert, 1879-1955. 2. Physicists.]
I. Title. II. Series.
QC16.E5B44   1996
530'.092—dc20   95-37500
                                              CIP

9 8 7 6 5 4 3 2 1

Printed in the United States of America
on acid-free paper

On the cover: *Albert Einstein in 1929;* Inset: *Einstein at his desk at the Swiss National Patent Office in Bern, 1905.*
Frontispiece: *Einstein in 1932, at the California Institute of Technology.*

Contents

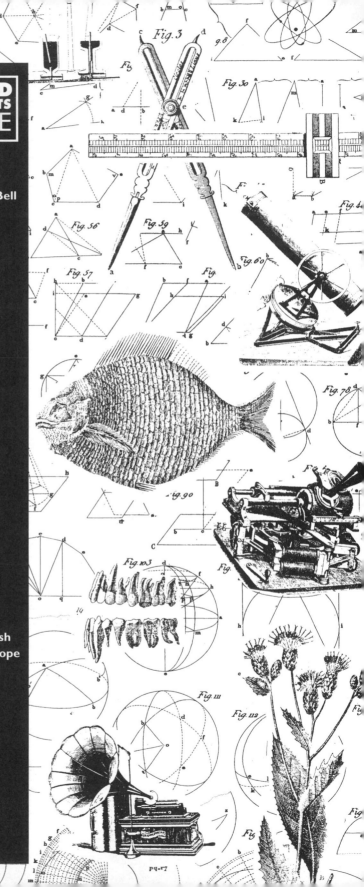

Oxford Portraits in Science

How I Did Not Get to Meet Albert Einstein

Many people who write biographies of famous people are at pains to tell the reader about how they met and spent time with their subject. In the best case this gives the reader a feeling of personal intimacy with the individual whose life is being described; in the worst case the reader may get the feeling that the book is really nothing but simpleminded hero-worshipping. Since I did not get to meet Albert Einstein I do not fall into either category. However, I thought by telling you how I did not get to meet Einstein I could introduce both myself and Einstein.

In 1947 I entered Harvard University as a freshman. I was 17 and had no intention of studying science. However, like many people I had heard of Einstein and his theory of relativity. Somehow I had learned that according to Einstein moving clocks slow down and that massive objects become more massive when observed in motion; indeed, that when such objects approach the speed of light they become so massive that they can no longer be accelerated at all. I had also read somewhere that space is "curved" and that there is a "fourth dimension," without having the slightest idea of what any of these terms meant. But to me the most interesting thing that I had read was that only seven people in the world understood the theory of relativity. This was very mysterious to me, and I became fascinated by the question of how so few people could understand something.

At the time I had a very limited view of what understanding something meant. In high school I had studied French and Spanish. Understanding Spanish meant translating it into English—which one could do, if necessary, with the help of a dictionary. We also studied poetry. Understanding poetry meant translating it into prose, which we also did, sometimes with the help of a dictionary. We also were taught to understand some mathematics. This meant being able to prove theorems and to manipulate symbols. Sometimes it meant memorizing the proofs of theorems. This may not have been "understanding" in the best sense of the term, but at least one could pass examinations.

From this limited experience it seemed to me that one could understand anything if only one took the time and effort and used the right "dictionaries." When one said then that only seven people in the world understood Einstein's theory of relativity, did that mean that only seven people were willing to put in the time and effort and that everyone else was too lazy, or did it mean something else? I was very intrigued by this question and, while still in high school, I began to acquire a crazy ambition. Though I did not want to become a scientist, the thought occurred to me that I might become the eighth person in the world to understand the theory of relativity—a challenge sort of like climbing Mount Everest. But how to go about it?

There was no one in my high school to guide me, so I forgot about relativity until I got to college. Fortunately for me, when I arrived at Harvard a new program was in place for teaching science to nonscientists. No longer did a nonscientist have to take a year's worth of one of the sciences, such as physics or chemistry. Instead he or she could take a "Natural Science" course that might treat several sciences and that would have a large historical part that would appeal to a nonscientist like myself. I looked through the course catalogue and hit upon Natural Sciences 3, which was taught by the historian of science I. Bernard Cohen. It appeared to be a survey course that began with the Greeks and ended up with the atomic bomb—which had been used on Hiroshima two years earlier. In this connection I had heard of Einstein's formula $E=mc^2$, although I had no real idea of what the symbols meant except that they had something to do with the atomic bomb. I was also told that Natural Sciences 3 was the easiest of the Natural Sciences courses, and being somewhat lazy and not a little intimidated by science I decided that this was the course for me.

Cohen was a comfortable sort of lecturer with clear round handwriting. As advertised, the course began with Greek astronomy and worked its way up to 20th-century physics. Just before Christmas, Cohen brought in a few of the ideas of Einstein. He presented various formulas of relativity and said that the derivations were too hard for our course. Then he said that only 12 people in the world really understood the theory. This statement caught my attention and I immediately remembered my old high school ambition. It is true that the number had since risen from 7 understanders to 12, but becoming the 13th wouldn't be bad either. I then hit on a scheme as to how I would go about this. I would go to Widener Library and look in the catalog under "Einstein." It went without saying, I reasoned, that he was one of the 12. I would then find a book he had written about the theory and I would read, say, a page a day until I understood it. It never dawned on me that anything else was required. This method seemed to work with poetry. Why not with relativity?

There were a few publications of Einstein's in the library. As luck would have it, I made the worst possible choice. The title appealed to me: *The Meaning of Relativity.* That had a nice philosophical ring to it. Unfortunately for me, as it turned out, it was a very technical book based on a series of lectures Einstein had given in Princeton in 1921 and then updated over the years. I did not realize this and simply began reading—very slowly. The first two paragraphs seemed all right. I shall reproduce them here since they give a flavor of Einstein's writing and also serve to introduce a few ideas. He begins:

> The theory of relativity is intimately connected with the theory of space and time. I shall therefore begin with a brief investigation of the origin of our ideas of space and time, although in doing so I know that I introduce a controversial subject. The object of all science, whether natural science or psychology, is to co-ordinate our experiences and to bring them into a logical system. How are our customary ideas of space and time related to the character of our experiences?

This I could understand, and I am sure you can, too. The next paragraph looked pretty good too. It read:

> The experiences of an individual appear to us arranged in a series of events; in this series the single events which we remember appear to be ordered according to the criterion of "earlier" and "later," which cannot be analyzed further. There exists, therefore, for the individual, an I-time, or subjective time. This in itself is not measurable. I can indeed associate numbers with the events, in such a way that a greater number is associated with the later event than with the earlier one; but the nature of this association is quite arbitrary. This association I can define by means of a clock by comparing the order of events furnished by the clock with the order of the given series of events which can be counted, and which has other properties we shall speak of later.

This paragraph, although a bit stickier than the first, I also thought I understood. In fact I found the idea of associating my personal sense of earlier and later with increasing numbers on a clock rather illuminating. I had never thought of things quite that way. But this was a whole page! In about an hour I had managed to understand a page. The book, not counting the appendices, was only 108 pages long! At the rate I was going, I figured, I could do the whole job in a month or so and become the 13th person to understand the theory. This worked, more or less, until page six, when I came across the following equation. I will reproduce it here as it appears in the book so you can get an idea of how I felt. Of course some of you may have already studied some advanced mathematics— in which case you will wonder how I could have been so ignorant. In any case here is the equation:

$$\Delta x'_\nu = \sum_\alpha \frac{\partial x'_\nu}{\partial x_\alpha} \Delta x_\alpha + \frac{1}{2} \sum_{\alpha\beta} \frac{\partial^2 x'_\nu}{\partial x_\alpha \partial x_\beta} \Delta x_\alpha \Delta x_\beta \cdots$$

I was completely stuck. No dictionary could help me. My whole project collapsed. Now that I have been studying Einstein's theory for so long I realize that the mathematics is the least of it. In this book I shall employ no advanced mathematics—nothing that a high school student would not have come across. Still, if I do my job right, by the time you finish reading the book you will come to understand the basic ideas of the theory of relativity and more besides. Of course, at the time I came across this equation, I understood none of this. I was hopelessly lost. I went to Professor Cohen for help. He made a suggestion that changed the course of my life, and I shall be forever grateful to him. He pointed out to me that in the spring a man named Philipp Frank would offer a course—a sort of slightly advanced Natural Sciences course—that dealt entirely with modern physics. He told me that Professor Frank was a good friend of Einstein's and had just published a biography called *Einstein: His Life and Times.* Professor Cohen said that while it was a little irregular for someone to take both his own course and the more advanced one at the same time, since I was so eager to understand relativity I should try it. I went out at once, bought Professor Frank's book, and enrolled in the course.

I was immensely curious as to how Professor Frank

might look. He was surely, after all, one of the sacred 13. I learned that the class was to be held in a big lecture auditorium in the physics building. It was the first time I had ever been to a physics building and I must say it looked rather depressing to me. It was dark and there were cabinets in the halls containing an apparently random collection of dusty bits of old apparatus. Whatever history they were supposed to represent was lost on me. In any event I went into the classroom and waited. At three o'clock Professor Frank teetered into the room. I say teetered because he had a significant limp, which I later learned had been caused by a childhood accident with a streetcar in his native Vienna. He was a short, ovoid man with a few grey hairs that stuck out at random from the sides of his bald top. He had a kindly, shrewd face that looked, I decided, like that of an extremely intelligent basset hound.

His accent was difficult to place. In the course of time I found that he spoke innumerable languages. French, German English, Italian, Spanish, Russian, Czech, some Hebrew, and Arabic were a few of them. The Czech had come about because in 1912 Professor Frank had succeeded Einstein as professor of physics in what was known as the German University in Prague, where Einstein had spent a year. The English had come about because in 1938 Professor Frank had emigrated to the United States from Czechoslovakia. The different languages were piled up one on top of each other like so many ruined cities—and that accounted for the accent.

Professor Frank turned out to have a wonderful sense of humor. So did Einstein, he later told me. He said that when Einstein was young he loved what Professor Frank in his inimitable accent called "cracks"—little jokes. (When Professor Frank said it, it sounded something like "kreks.") I can see the two of them—Einstein and Professor Frank— then young men in their 20s in the coffeehouses that they frequented, telling jokes and laughing. It is not the image one usually has of Einstein as a white-haired sage. One forgets how he must have seemed as a young man.

The course covered some of the same material that Cohen had gone over, beginning with the geometry of the ancient Greeks. I still have the notes that I took in what is now an old, worn, leatherbound notebook. Professor Frank was not really a historian, so I am not sure how reliable his dates and places were. But he was able to reveal what things meant. When it came to Newton he made me understand for the first time what the famous story about the falling of the apple really meant. He told us that Newton was performing a "thought experiment"—the kind of thing that Einstein was an absolute master of—in which one imagines a situation that is impossible to carry out in practice, but that is possible in principle and that reveals a new idea in physics—the power of pure thought. Newton as a young man watched the falling of an apple from a tree in an orchard near where he lived. He imagined, Professor Frank told us, that the tree kept growing so that it stretched from here to the Moon. Then he could think of the Moon as an apple on the branch of a huge tree. It, too, would be falling like the apple in the orchard, influenced by the Earth's gravity. This led Newton to the idea that gravity is "universal"—that it acts on everything, everywhere, and that one of the components of the Moon's motion is that it is continually "falling" towards the Earth like a falling apple.

Professor Frank taught us that there were geometries that the Greeks had not imagined—and that these played an important role in Einstein's view of gravitation. His arguments never involved higher mathematics but rather a careful step-by-step understanding. I will present some of them to you later in this book. But I also came to realize something else. So long as I did not learn more mathematics and physics I would never really understand the theory of relativity. By this time it was clear to me that the idea that there were only, say, 12 people in the world who understood relativity had been a sort of joke. Every working physicist had to have a good understanding of the theory, and there were many physicists—"relativists" they were called—who had spent their lives working on it. But to advance to the next level of understanding I would have to begin the very difficult job of learning the basics.

While still far from deciding to become a physicist, I decided in my sophomore year to learn enough mathematics and physics so that I could take the next step in my understanding. I took freshman physics as a sophomore, as well as beginning calculus. I also took another course with Professor Frank and began to get to know him. By the spring of my sophomore year I had another crazy idea. I would go to Princeton to the Institute for Advanced Study and talk to Einstein. I don't remember what I thought I would speak to him about. Now if only I had had that chance there are so many things I would like to have asked him that I hardly know where to begin. I wrote him a letter. I suppose he must have gotten hundreds like it. I doubt that he would have answered, except that as it happened Professor Frank was going to Princeton to see him and he said he would discuss the matter with Einstein. Much to my astonishment, in early June Einstein wrote me a letter. I framed it and I am looking at it as I write this. It is dated June 3, 1949, and was sent from his home at 112 Mercer Street in Princeton, an address that was world-famous while he was alive and that I visited some years after his death in 1955. It reads:

> Dear Mr. Bernstein:
>
> I am sending you enclosed paper in which I expressed opinions from an epistological point of view. [I didn't know exactly what "epistological" meant but the paper was about his philosophy of science.] I do not give oral interviews to avoid misinterpretation.
>
> Sincerely yours.
> A. Einstein

That is the story of how I didn't get to meet Albert Einstein.

Albert Einstein at age five with his sister Maria. In a short biographical sketch of her brother, Maria reminisced about the young Einstein's occasional temper tantrums.

Einstein When Young

Albert Einstein was born on March 15, 1879, in the south-
ern German city of Ulm, at the foot of the Swabian Alps.
The house where he was born, 135 Bahnhofstrasse, was
destroyed in a bombing raid during World War II. Both of
his parents, Hermann and Pauline Koch Einstein, were
Jewish, although they did not strictly practice the religion.
The fact that they gave their son Albert and his sister Maria,
who was born two years later, traditional German names
rather than Old Testament names, such as Abraham and
Sarah, shows that they had moved away from Orthodox
Judaism. Nonetheless, their religious affiliation, "Israelitic,"
was printed on Einstein's birth certificate, and it is interesting in light of this to speculate about what it might have
meant for the history of modern science had Einstein been
born a half century earlier or later in the same German city.

Until 1871, only eight years before Einstein's birth,
Jews had not been considered full citizens of Germany; they
did not have the same rights and opportunities as other
Germans. Indeed, earlier in the century they had been
forced to live in ghettos and were frequently required to
wear special yellow badges—a practice revived by the Nazis

some 50 years after Einstein's birth. Jews were not allowed to attend universities and could practice only a very limited number of professions. Hence, if someone of Einstein's ability had been born in such a ghetto at that time, he would either have gone unnoticed or might have become a religious scholar. Examples of Jewish scientists in Europe, at least any whose work is widely recognized, seem nonexistent before the middle of the 19th century. Consequently, it is not surprising that there is no record of anyone in either Einstein's mother's or father's family showing outstanding scientific ability.

Of course, on the other hand, had Einstein been born 50 years later, his birth would have coincided with the rise of Nazism in Germany, and if he had not been one of the few Jews lucky enough to emigrate, he would have perished in a concentration camp. Even so, he was forced to leave Germany in 1932, never to return. Apart from this, being born in 1879 meant that he was in his early 20s at the turn of the century, when the traditional "classical" physics of Isaac Newton and his successors was breaking down. It took a revolution to fix physics, and revolutions are usually made, certainly in physics, by people under the age of 30. Hence Einstein was just at the right age to look at things with a fresh eye. He had no stake in the established physics.

After Einstein had become famous, his sister Maria— who was nicknamed Maja—wrote a short biographical sketch of her older brother, to whom she was very close. She described how Einstein appeared to her when they were both babies. She recalled that he had had occasional temper tantrums when "his face would turn pale, the tip of his nose would become white, and he would lose control of himself." It is generally agreed that young Albert took a very long time before he began to speak. Late in life Einstein recalled this, and he told one of his assistants that at age two or three he had acquired the ambition to speak in whole sentences and would practice them silently to himself until he was sure that he had gotten them right before saying them aloud. Surely few adults can remember how they learned to speak. But by the time he was an adult, and universally recognized as the greatest scientific genius since Newton, Einstein had been asked so often how his mental processes differed from most people's that he had thought a good deal about how they had developed. That is probably why he remembered, or thought he remembered, how he had learned to speak.

Einstein's mother loved music, and so her two children were given music lessons when they were very young. Einstein began playing the violin when he was 6 and took lessons until he was 13. He played regularly until old age, when he came to feel that it was too difficult for him to play anymore. It is not clear just how good a violinist he was. All sorts of famous musicians wanted to, and did, accompany him, but they probably did so because he was Einstein the physicist and not Einstein the musician.

Einstein's interest in music also led to some other interesting friendships. Beginning in 1911, a wealthy and somewhat eccentric Belgian industrialist named Ernest Solvay organized and paid for conferences held from time to time in the Belgian capital of Brussels. Solvay had some odd scientific ideas, and he probably thought that if he paid them enough he could assemble a group of distinguished scientists to listen to him. Once gathered, however, the scientists preferred to listen to each other. It was during these meetings that Einstein got to know the king and queen of Belgium, whom he referred to as the "Kings," as if that were their last name. Einstein wrote to his wife from Brussels in 1930:

> At 3 o'clock I drove out to the Kings where I was received with touching warmth. These people are of a purity and kindness seldom found. First we talked for about an hour. Then an English woman musician arrived, and we played quartets and trios (a musical lady-in-waiting was also present). This went on merrily for several hours. Then they all

went away and I stayed behind alone for dinner with the Kings—vegetarian style, no servants. Spinach with hard-boiled eggs and potatoes, period. (It had not been anticipated that I would stay.) I liked it very much there, and I am certain the feeling was mutual.

Einstein's father, Hermann, was not very successful in business. When Albert was a year old, his father decided to begin an electrical engineering and plumbing enterprise with his younger brother Jakob, who had studied engineering. They set up their business in the large German city of Munich with the financial help of Pauline Einstein's parents. The young Albert spent the next 14 years of his life in Munich and got his elementary school education there. At that time in Germany, most of the state-supported schools had a religious affiliation. There were Jewish schools, Catholic schools, and so on. Einstein's parents decided that he would get a better general education in the Catholic school and so he went there. He was the only Jew in his school, but this did not seem to pose any problems for him.

However, these schools also had a military tradition and often a military atmosphere, which was something that Einstein hated from the beginning. As a child he had never played with soldiers, and he watched military parades with a feeling of pity and contempt. These feelings lasted for much of his life. During World War I Einstein even got into trouble as an antiwar activist. Only in the 1930s, with the rise of Adolf Hitler in Germany, did Einstein change his views, coming to the conclusion that Hitler could be stopped only by force.

There is no evidence that during his years in Munich Einstein impressed any of his teachers as having any special talent. Several great theoretical physicists have shown remarkable abilities—often in mathematics—at a very early age, learning calculus before reaching their teens or showing exceptional ability in performing mental arithmetic, but Einstein does not appear to have done any of these things.

In fact, he impressed his early teachers as a dreamy child without an especially promising future. Nonetheless, Einstein tells us, his first strong scientific memories date from this time. Einstein never did write an autobiography of the kind that many scientists now do write, in which they tell us of their marriages, their children, and even their love affairs, and sometimes their work in science. Though Einstein was married twice, had three children, and very likely did have love affairs, he must have felt strongly that this was his own business, because when he did write an autobiographical essay at age 67, he included almost nothing about his personal life. He did not even tell us whether he had been married. The essay is almost entirely concerned with the origins of his scientific ideas. It is from this "autobiography" that we learn when and how science entered Einstein's life.

In his essay, Einstein has two very distinct childhood scientific memories to tell us about. They relate closely to the kind of science he was later to do. He describes these memories in terms of the sense of wonder they produced in

Einstein, front row, third from right, with his classmates in Munich, 1889. Einstein hated his school's harsh, military atmosphere.

him. "Wonder" is a very important word here. We all wonder about things we observe in nature around us. What holds the clouds up? Why are there seasons? What makes water boil, plants green, or the sky blue? The scientist differs from other people in that he or she cannot stand not knowing the answer to questions like this. Such an individual will stay up all night—even many nights—until the question is resolved. Einstein felt so strongly about this drive that he referred to it as the "flight from wonder." It is as if the scientist is fleeing from wonder—the feeling of not understanding something—a feeling that for a scientist is dreadful, even terrifying, and can only be relieved by coming to understand it.

Einstein's first scientific memory was of his father showing him a compass when he was about five. Describing the seemingly strange phenomenon of the compass needle's "knowing" where to point even though nothing appears to be touching it, he writes, "That this needle behaved in such a determined way did not at all fit into the nature of events...in the unconscious world of concepts...." He continues, "I can still remember—or at least I believe I can remember—that this experience made a deep and lasting impression on me. Something deeply hidden had to be behind things...." If such an experience is to be different from magic, then the scientist must find out why it happens and how it relates to more familiar things. It is striking that Einstein's first childhood scientific memory had to do with magnetism, since many years later one of the triumphs of his relativity theory was to show how magnetism and electricity are really a single phenomenon that is usually called electromagnetism.

But at the time of Einstein's childhood experience, the modern theory of electromagnetism was still in its own childhood. It had been developed by the great Scottish physicist James Clerk Maxwell some 25 years earlier, and when Einstein got his real scientific education around the turn of the century, the concept of electromagnetism was still so new and understood by so few people that it was not even taught in his classes. He had to teach it to himself.

The second scientific experience Einstein recalled was of a quite different character. It involved geometry and occurred when he was about 12. By this time he had passed from the elementary school to what was known as a Gymnasium. This was really a high school, but at a very serious level. Some of the Gymnasium teachers were scholars in their own right who had published books or done significant scientific experimentation. Einstein went to the Luitpold Gymnasium in Munich, a Catholic school where the discipline seemed even more military than at his elementary school. A picture of him taken with his classmates—all boys—shows them wearing uniforms. It might as well have been a military school. In fact, Einstein referred to his teachers as "lieutenants," as opposed to the "sergeants" who taught in his elementary school. In the picture he seems to be expressing a smirk and looks like the kind of boy who might well drive a teacher somewhat crazy. This was not far from the truth.

By the time Einstein had these early scientific experiences, he was already beginning to read popular books on science. They had been suggested to him by a poor Jewish student from Russia named Max Talmud. Though the Einsteins were not formally very religious, they did follow the Jewish custom of inviting a poor scholar to dine with them—in Talmud's case, every Thursday at noon. Among the books that Talmud suggested to Einstein were a few by an author named Aaron Bernstein, who had written a series entitled *Popular Books on Natural Science*. Talmud and Einstein used to spend hours discussing these books.

In addition, Einstein's uncle Jakob encouraged his budding interest in mathematics and often presented problems in algebra or geometry for him to solve. One of these problems was to prove the Pythagorean theorem in plane geom-

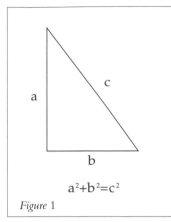

a

c

b

$a^2+b^2=c^2$

Figure 1

etry, which states that the sum of the squared values of the two legs of a right triangle is equal to the squared value of the hypotenuse. Next his uncle gave him a book on geometry, so that Einstein could see how the subject was organized. Einstein later wrote, "At the age of 12 I experienced a second wonder of a totally different nature: in a little book dealing with Euclidean plane geometry, which came into my hands at the beginning of the school year. Here were assertions which—although by no means evident—could nevertheless be proved with such certainty that any doubt appeared to be out of the question. This lucidity and certainty made an indescribable impression upon me. That the axiom had to be accepted unproved did not disturb me. I could peg proofs upon propositions the validity of which did not seem dubious...."

Here Einstein is sharing something that probably all of us have felt about geometry. It is the amazing fact that if we begin from a few seemingly self-evident propositions—known as axioms—such as the possibility of connecting any two points with a straight line, or that all right angles are equal to each other, we can prove remarkable theorems. We are all taught that we cannot "prove" the axioms themselves. We must accept them as the building blocks from which we will construct the theorems of geometry. Einstein then goes on to tell us how he tried to do this with the Pythagorean theorem. Here is what he says: "I remember that an uncle [Jakob] told me the Pythagorean theorem before the holy geometry booklet had come into my hands. After much effort I succeeded in 'proving' this theorem on the basis of similarity of triangles; in doing so it seemed to me 'evident' that the relations of the sides of right-angled triangles would have to be completely determined by one of the acute angles. Only something which did not in similar fashion seem to be 'evident' appeared to me to be in need of any proof at all...." The box on page 26 presents what Einstein's proof must have been, but this is somewhat of a guess, since he does not give us any more details.

In 1894, Hermann Einstein moved his family—except for Albert—to Milan in Italy. Business had not been good in Munich and the firm's Italian representative suggested that the Einstein brothers might try their luck in his country. Albert was left behind to finish his Gymnasium education. He stayed in a boardinghouse run by a distant relative. By this time the whole atmosphere of the Gymnasium had begun to weigh heavily on his nerves. It is sometimes said that Einstein was a poor student. He wasn't. He was by and large an excellent student—perhaps not at the top of his class all the time—but he had very good grades. However, he was not a very respectful student, and this became clear to his teachers.

In any event, after six months of living on his own in Munich, Einstein decided to escape. He managed to get a note from a doctor saying that he was suffering from a nervous breakdown. He also got a note from a mathematics teacher to the effect that his superior knowledge of mathematics had prepared him for more advanced work. However, all of this became academic when he was summoned by a teacher who informed him that he was being asked to leave the school. When he inquired why, he was told, "Your presence in the class destroys the respect of the students." One has only to look at the picture of Einstein with his class to understand what the teacher might have had in mind. But this worked out splendidly for Einstein. If he had stayed the full year he would have become old enough to be drafted.

Since he had not bothered to inform his parents in advance about his move, it must have come as something of a surprise when he appeared in Italy. It came as more of a surprise when Einstein announced that he was giving up his German citizenship. On this he was adamant. Under no

text continues on page 29

I n this box I will give you my understanding of what Einstein was saying about the Pythagorean theorem. This will also give us a chance to review the theorem, which we will use later when we discuss some of the predictions of Einstein's theory of relativity.

Below I have drawn two right triangles of different sizes—a big one and a small one.

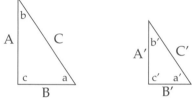

Figure 2

I have labeled the sides of the triangles respectively A, B, C, and A′, B′, and C′. The sides C and C′ are the hypotenuses of the two triangles. I call a, b, and c the angles opposite the sides A, B, and C, and likewise a′, b′, and c′ for the small triangle. Since these are right triangles both c and c′ are 90°. Recall that the sum of the angles of any triangle is 180°. Thus, if, for example, the angle a is equal to the angle a′, then we must also have the angle b equal to the angle b′. This follows from the equations a+b=90° and a′+b′=90° so that a+b=a′+b′. Thus if one of the acute angles of a right triangle is equal to one of the acute angles of another right triangle, all the angles are equal and the two triangles are what are called "similar." This definition of similar triangles implies another one. If all the angles are equal, then corresponding sides are proportional to each other. In equations this says that

$$\frac{A}{A'} = \frac{B}{B'} = \frac{C}{C'}$$

If you know some trigonometry you can easily see this from the sines and cosines of the angles a and a′ when you let these angles be equal. Remember that the sine of an angle is the ratio of the length of the side opposite the angle to the hypotenuse while the cosine is the ratio of the length of the side adjacent to the angle to the hypotenuse. I do not know if Einstein knew any trigonometry when he was twelve, but this is what he meant when he wrote "it seemed to me 'evident' that the relations of the sides of the right-angled triangles would have to be completely determined by one of the acute angles."

Going from this understanding to a proof of the Pythagorean theorem is not very long once we draw the correct diagram. Once again we consider a right triangle with the sides and angles labeled as before.

Figure 3

Next we drop a line that hits C at right angles as shown in the next figure.

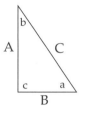

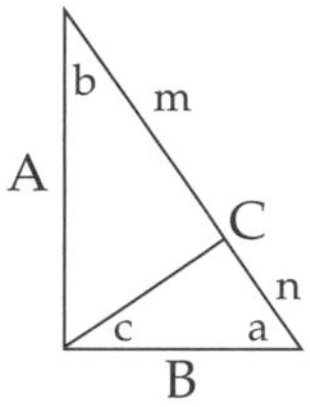

Figure 4

Now we have three triangles; two small ones and the big one we started with. But these three triangles are all similar to each other. In the next figure I have put in all the angles and labeled the two lines that form the bases of the little triangles m and n. It is clear from the relation of these triangles that m+n=C. Now we can use the proportionality of the various sides of the similar triangles to conclude the equations

$$\frac{A}{C} = \frac{n}{A} \qquad \text{and} \qquad \frac{B}{C} = \frac{m}{B}$$

continues on page 28

text continued from page 27

But these equations are just the Pythagorean theorem in disguise. We can multiply up and rewrite them as

$$A^2 = n \times C,$$

and

$$B^2 = m \times C$$

If we add the equations we have the Pythagorean theorem

$$A^2 + B^2 = (m+n)\, C = C^2$$

The last step follows from the fact that

$$m + n = C$$

I think this is what Einstein meant when he said "After much effort I succeeded in 'proving' this theorem on the basis of the similarity of triangles."

text continued from page 25

circumstances would he remain a German national. It was not entirely clear what this meant in practical terms, but for the next six months he had a wonderful time wandering around Italy on his own. But for Einstein, who was then 16, wandering did not mean playing the guitar and singing in cafes of Italy for the odd lira as he went from place to place soaking up the culture. In the first place, he was already bitten by the "physics bug." He wanted to learn how nature worked. It is unlikely that he knew what a professional physicist was, but he did have the idea that he might become a science teacher. His father thought he should become an electrical engineer, which would at least be a profession at which he could earn a living.

As it happened, the best place in Europe in which to study science and engineering, outside of Germany, was the Swiss Federal Institute of Technology in Zurich. The school is often referred to as the ETH, the abbreviation for its German name, *Eidgenossische Technische Hochschule*. The ETH had several things to recommend it in addition to the fact that it was not located in Germany. On its faculty were several scientists and mathematicians of world renown, which is always a good recommendation. It also did not require a high school diploma for entry; instead, applicants had to pass a difficult entrance examination. Finally—and this would play an important part in the next stage of Einstein's life—it admitted women.

Einstein was just 16 ½ when he took the entrance examination, about a year and a half younger than the average student. Moreover, he had not bothered especially to prepare for the examination—which was typical of him at that time. Hence it is not surprising that he failed the part of the examination that dealt with languages. Fortunately for both Einstein and for physics, the principal of the ETH, Albin Herzog—to whom we owe a debt of gratitude for saving Einstein's academic career—recognized some spark of a mathematical gift in Einstein and proposed a plan by

Einstein in 1893, while he was a student at the ETH in Munich.

which he might eventually get into the ETH. According to the plan, Einstein was to spend a year studying both languages and science in a high school in Aarau, a few miles from Zurich. This was a progressive school with an excellent reputation for science teaching. It was a wonderful decision, and Einstein spent one of the happiest and most fruitful years of his life in Aarau.

It was there that he clarified his ambition to engage in science. At one point, probably for a French class, he wrote a brief statement about his future plans. The little paper still exists. Translated from Einstein's schoolboy French, it reads:

My plans for the future

A happy man is too content with the present to think much about the future. Young people, on the other hand, like to occupy themselves with bold plans. Furthermore, it is natural for a serious young man to gain as precise an idea as possible about his desired aims.

If I were to have the good fortune to pass my examinations I would go to the [ETH] in Zurich. I would stay there for four years in order to study mathematics and physics. I imagine myself becoming a teacher in those branches of the natural sciences, choosing the theoretical part of them.

Here are the reasons which led me to this plan. Above all, it is [my] disposition for abstract and mathematical thought, [my] lack of imagination and practical ability. My desires have also inspired in me the same resolve. That is quite natural; one always likes to do the things for which one has the ability. Then there is also a certain independence in the scientific profession which I like a great deal.

Apart from the stimulating atmosphere of the school at Aarau, at which Einstein got the opportunity to do a good deal of hands-on scientific experimentation, he had a very pleasant boarding arrangement. He lived with the Winteler family, of whom the "Papa," named Winteler-Jost, was a teacher at the school whom Einstein respected and liked. Interestingly, in 1910, Einstein's sister Maja married Paul Winteler, one of his sons. With his school year underway, Einstein finally persuaded his father to write to the authorities of the German state of Württemburg—at that time one was a citizen of a state and not the entire country—to withdraw his citizenship. This was done, and upon the payment of three German marks Einstein received, at the beginning of 1896, documents confirming it. He remained stateless—a man without an official country—until 1901, when he became a Swiss citizen. However, it is well known that although Switzerland has remained a neutral country during the wars of this century, it is a country with compulsory military service for men. In fact, Swiss men serve part-time in the army for much of their lives. This did not seem to bother Einstein at all. He was quite prepared, upon becoming a Swiss citizen, to serve in the army like everyone else, but he was turned down for having flat feet. In the fall of 1896, after graduating from his high school in Aarau, Einstein was admitted to the ETH to begin a four-year program that would qualify him as a teacher of mathematics and physics.

Looking back after these many years one is led to think that Einstein's four-year stay at the ETH was neither a great success nor a great failure. Something of this impression enters into the tone of Einstein's reminiscences in his autobiography. He writes that while at the ETH, "I had excellent teachers...so that I really could have gotten a sound mathematical education. However, I worked most of the time in the physical laboratory, fascinated by the direct contact with experience. The balance of time I used in the main to study at home...." Examinations, however, remained mandatory, and here Einstein expresses his unhappiness: "The hitch in all of this was...that one had to cram all this stuff into one's mind for the examinations whether one liked it or not. This coercion had such a deterring effect [upon me] that, after I had passed the final examinations, I found the consideration of any scientific problems distasteful to me for an entire year." Nevertheless, he observes that "In justice I must add...that in Switzerland we had to suffer far less under such coercion, which smothers every truly scientific impulse, than is the case in many another locality. There were altogether only two examinations; aside from these, one could just about do as one pleased. This was especially the case if one had a friend, as did I, who attended lectures regularly and who worked over their content conscientiously. This gave one freedom in the choice of pursuits until a few months before the examination, a freedom I enjoyed to a great extent and have gladly taken into the bargain the bad conscience connected with it as by far the lesser evil."

Discussing the coercive effect of obligatory study, Einstein calls it "nothing short of a miracle that the modern methods of instruction have not yet strangled the holy curiosity of inquiry, for this delicate little plant, aside from stimulation, stands mainly in need of freedom; without which it goes to wreck and ruin without fail. It is a very grave mistake to think that the enjoyment of seeing and searching can be promoted by means of coercion and a sense of duty."

In one sense, this may seem a profound observation, but in another, it can be perceived as highly elitist. Few people can teach themselves more physics than they can be taught—especially at the beginning. Physics is a very difficult subject, and to learn it, most of us need guidance and discipline. We need contact with our fellow researchers and with experimental reality, or we can easily lose our way.

Who the "friend" was who went to his classes at the ETH and took scrupulous notes, Einstein does not tell us, but it may have been his girlfriend and future wife, Mileva Maric. (Another likely candidate was a fellow student named Marcel Grossman, who was known to have taken meticulous notes and who later collaborated with Einstein on some of the mathematics that led to Einstein's theory of gravitation.) One of the most complicated questions that confronts any biographer of Einstein is his relationship to women. Throughout much of his life, and especially in his early years, Einstein was a very good-looking man who appealed to women. It is also quite likely that for a woman, living with him was not easy. For Einstein, physics came first and individual human relationships were of much less importance. He seemed much more interested in humanity generally than in the individual human beings who constituted it. This is not to say that Einstein was incapable of falling in love. Indeed, as we shall see, he was certainly deeply in love, at least in the beginning, with Mileva Maric. But something—what might almost seem a guilty conscience—haunted him all his life about his relationships with women.

Clear evidence of this appears in one of the last letters Einstein ever wrote. It is dated March 21, 1955, less than a month before Einstein died on April 18th. It is written to the son and the sister of the man who seemed to have been Einstein's closest friend, a Swiss-born engineer named Michele Besso. In this remarkable letter Einstein writes:

> Dear Vero and Dear Mme. Bice:
>
> It was truly good of you to give me, in those so painful days, so many details concerning the death of Michele. His end was in harmony with the image of his entire life and the image of the circle of people that surrounded him. The gift of leading a harmonious life is rarely joined to such a keen intelligence, especially to the degree one found in him. But what I admired most about Michele was the fact that he was able to live so many years with one woman, not only in peace but also in constant unity, something I have lamentably failed at twice....

However it ended, Einstein's relationship with Mileva Maric began as a love affair. Mileva had been born in Hungary in 1875, making her some four years older than Einstein. She was also a Catholic, and although the religious difference was of no importance to Einstein and of apparently no great importance to Maric's family, it was of great importance to Einstein's parents and one of several reasons they gave for not liking her. It is unclear what impelled her to come to Zurich to study physics, except that the ETH was one of the rare places in Europe at which a woman could study science of any kind. Studying physics is not a common thing for women to do even today, and before the turn of the century it must have been an act of devotion bordering on heroism. For many years very little was known about Einstein's relationship with Mileva except that it eventually ended in divorce. In the past decade, however, an entire set of letters exchanged between Einstein and Mileva, beginning in 1897—a year after Einstein entered the ETH—has come to light and been published.

By the fall of 1897, Einstein and Mileva appear to have already become rather good friends. In October of that year, while visiting her family in Hungary, she wrote, "My father gave me some tobacco to take with me and I was supposed to hand it to you, he wanted so much to whet your appetite for our little country of brigands. [Einstein was a great pipe smoker for much of his life until, near the end of it, his doctor forbade him to buy tobacco. He got around this by "stealing" it from colleagues.] I talked with him about you, you absolutely must come with me someday. The marvelous conversations you would have here! But I will take over the role of interpreter. But I cannot send it [the tobacco] to you, you would have to pay duty on it, and then you would curse me along with my present...."

Apparently, Mileva stayed in Hungary longer than Einstein expected, and from the next letter he wrote to her, in February 1898, it seems that she might not have returned at all. In this letter, Einstein writes, "I am very happy about your intention to continue your studies here again. I am sure you will not regret it. I am quite convinced that you will be able to catch up in a relatively short time with the main courses we had. To be sure, it puts me in a very embarrassing position if I have to tell you what material we covered. Simply it's only here that you will find the material properly arranged and elucidated...." By the following August the relationship had progressed: Einstein's letters no longer began with "Dear Miss" but with "Dear D," "D" being an abbreviation for "Doxerl," a term of endearment. The letters also begin to reveal Einstein's developing ideas in physics.

By October 1898 Einstein was discussing "our household," as if he and Mileva were sharing living quarters. By a year later it is clear that Einstein had decided to marry Mileva, and describes in a letter to her what seems to have become a familiar argument with his mother.

> We come home, I into Mama's room (just the two of us). First I have to tell her about the examination. [This was the graduation examination from the ETH, which Einstein passed with good but far from outstanding grades. Mileva failed the examination and failed it again the following year, which seems to have been the last time she tried to get her degree from the ETH.] Then she asks me quite innocently: "So, what will become of Dockerl? [another spelling of Doxerl]" "My wife," say I equally innocently, but prepared for a real "scene." This then ensued immediately. Mama threw herself on the bed, buried her head in the pillow and cried like a child. After she had recovered from the initial shock, she immediately switched to a desperate offensive, "You are ruining your future and blocking your path through life. That woman cannot gain entrance to a decent family. If she gets a child you'll be in a pretty mess." At this last outburst, which had been preceded by several others, my patience finally gave out. I rejected the suspicion that we had been living in sin with all my might, scolded properly & was just ready to leave the room, when Mama's friend Mrs. Bar entered the room, a

small, lively little woman full of life, such a sort of hen of the nicest kind. Thereupon we immediately started to talk with the greatest eagerness about the weather, new spa guests, ill-behaved children, etc. Then we went to eat, after that we played some music. When we said good night to each other in private, the same story started again, but "piu piano" [more quietly].

On the next day, Einstein writes, matters had improved, and his mother said, "'If they have not yet had intimate relations (so much dreaded by her) and will wait so long, then ways and means will be found.' Only what is most terrible for her is that we want to stay together always. Her attempts at converting me were based on speeches like: 'She is a book like you—but you ought to have a wife.' 'When you'll be thirty, she'll be and old hag,' etc. But as she sees that in the meantime she is accomplishing nothing except to make me angry, she has given up the 'treatment' for the time being."

There is no reason to doubt Einstein's truthfulness in telling his mother that at the time of this letter he and Mileva were not intimately involved. The letter was written in July 1900. A year and half later, things had changed radically. Einstein and Mileva still had not married, largely because Einstein had been unable to find a job. But in a letter written to Mileva on December 12, 1901, he makes it clear that he knows she is pregnant. He writes, almost as an aside, "Take good care of yourself and be cheerful and rejoice in our dear Lieserl [an affectionate rendering of Lise], whom I in absolute secrecy, to be sure (so that Doxerl wouldn't notice it) prefer to think of as Hanserl [a correspondingly affectionate rendering of Hans]." Einstein sent this letter and the ones that follow to Mileva in Hungary, to which she had returned to be with her parents when she had her baby. There is no indication that Einstein's family or anyone else close to him, even Besso, had any idea of any of this. In fact, no one outside Mileva's family suspected it until Einstein's letters to her appeared in the late 1980s.

The baby, a girl, appears to have been born in late January or early February 1899, because on February 4th of that year, Einstein wrote Mileva,

> My beloved sweetheart!
>
> Poor, dear sweetheart, you must suffer enormously if you cannot even write to me yourself! And our dear Lieserl too must get to know the world from this aspect right from the beginning! I hope that you will be up and around again by the time my letter arrives. I was scared out of my wits when I got your father's letter, because I had already suspected some trouble....But you see, it has really turned out to be a Lieserl, as you wished. Is she healthy and does she already cry properly? What kind of little eyes does she have? Whom of us two does she resemble more? Who is giving her milk? Is she hungry? And so she is completely bald? I love her so much & I don't even know her yet! Couldn't she be photographed once you are totally healthy again? Will she soon be able to turn her eyes toward something? Now you can make observations. I would like once to produce a Lierserl myself, it must be so interesting! She certainly can cry already, but to laugh she'll learn much later. Therein lies a profound truth. When you feel a little better, you must make a drawing of her....

There is no reason to doubt the sincerity of the feelings Einstein was expressing here. On the other hand the letter was written from Switzerland to Hungary, and whatever his feelings, Einstein did not seem impelled to make the voyage himself. In fact, it is probable that he never saw a photograph of Lieserl, who has disappeared without a trace. Did she get sick and die? Was she put up for adoption? If so, what happened to her? No one has been able to find out.

The Miracle Year

The first *annus mirabilis,* or miracle year, in physics was 1665. That was the year in which Isaac Newton retreated from Cambridge University to his mother's house in Lincolnshire, England, to avoid the Great Plague that was ravishing population centers such as London and Cambridge. He was 24 years old, and as he later reminisced, "in those days [I was]...in the prime of my age for invention and minded [thought about] mathematicks and philosophy [natural science] more than at any time since." During the succeeding 18 months Newton created the physics, and the mathematics for it, that dominated the subject for the next 250 years. Many of the things Newton discovered during that time were not revealed for many years thereafter. He was a very secretive man who greatly feared that his work would be stolen and credit given to others. Finally, in 1686, his masterpiece—the *Principia*—was published. It was a very difficult book, written in Latin and making use of very complicated geometrical arguments. Nonetheless, enough people understood enough of the *Principia* to make it clear to the less knowledgeable that Newton had created an entire world system. It appeared as if Newton's laws, which

SECT. III.

De motu Corporum in Conicis Sectionibus excentricis.

Prop. XI. Prob. VI.

Revolvatur corpus in Ellipsi: Requiritur lex vis centripetæ tendentis ad umbilicum Ellipseos.

Esto Ellipseos superioris umbilicus S. Agatur *SP* secans Ellipseos tum diametrum *DK* in *E*, tum ordinatim applicatam *Q v* in *x*, & compleatur parallelogrammum *Q x P R*. Patet *E P* æqualem esse semiaxi majori *AC*, eo quod acta ab altero Ellipseos umbilico *H I* ipsi *E C* parallela, (ob æquales *C S, C H*) æquentur *ES, EI*, adeo ut *EP* semisumma sit ipsarum *PS*

adæquant. Ad *SP* demittatur
eos latere recto principali (seu
Q R ad *L* x P *v* ut *Q R* ad *P v*;
& *L* x P *v* ad *G v* P ut *L* ad *G v*;
&

PHILOSOPHIÆ
NATURALIS
PRINCIPIA
MATHEMATICA.

Autore *J S. NEWTON*, Trin. Coll. Cantab. Soc. Matheseos Professore *Lucasiano*, & Societatis Regalis Sodali.

IMPRIMATUR·
S. PEPYS, *Reg. Soc.* PRÆSES.
Julii 5. 1686.

LONDINI,

Jussu *Societatis Regiæ* ac Typis *Josephi Streater*. Prostat apud plures Bibliopolas. *Anno* MDCLXXXVII.

The scientific principles set out by Isaac Newton in his Principia, published in 1686, dominated physics for more than 200 years—until Einstein came along.

originated from a few simple principles, were enough to determine the entire past and future of the universe. For the next 250 years, physicists spent their time elaborating the Newtonian system. It never seemed to occur to anyone—at least until Einstein—that Newton's laws might actually be wrong.

What would Newton and Einstein find to say to each other if they were to meet today? They did have a few things in common. Both made their fundamental discoveries at about the same age. Newton was 24 and Einstein, in the "miracle year" of 1905, was 26. Apart from their "genius," both men also had the capacity to focus on a problem for years, simply refusing to give up. It took Newton many years before he was satisfied with his calculations of the motion of the Moon, and it took Einstein 10 years—from 1905 to 1915—to create the theory that would replace Newton's. Moreover, both men came from a condition of obscurity to become the symbols of their age. But no two men could have been more different.

Take the matter of religion. Einstein's first exposure to organized religion was in the Catholic grammar school in Munich. He was, at the time, more religious than his family, taking what the New Testament said as the literal truth. Then he discovered science. What happened next he describes in his autobiography: "Through the reading of popular science books I soon reached [a] conviction that much in the stories of the Bible could not be true. The consequence was a positively fanatic [orgy of] freethinking coupled with the impression that youth is intentionally being deceived by the state through lies: it was a crushing impression. Suspicion against every kind of authority grew out of this experience, a skeptical attitude towards the convictions that were alive in any specific social environment—an attitude which has never again left me, even though later on, because of a better insight into the causal connections, it lost some of its original poignancy."

In other words, Einstein's contact with science made him question every sort of authority, including religious authority. This is not to say that he was not a religious man, although perhaps "spiritual" is a better word. After he became famous, Einstein was frequently asked if he believed in God. In answering, he always made a distinction between a "personal" God who listened to and answered our individual prayers and God as represented by the organization of the universe: the fact that the universe seemed to obey definite laws and that these could be understood by humankind. In the spirit of this distinction Einstein did not believe in a personal God, but he very much believed in a larger organizing spirit in the universe. Einstein often spoke of this spirit, sometimes calling it "the Old One." He often said the real business of physics was to uncover the secrets of the "Old One," and he felt that ultimately these secrets would turn out to be simple, and the laws that govern the universe beautiful. He believed that God would not be so nasty as to produce ugly laws, and as he once said, "God is subtle, but not malicious."

Isaac Newton was only 24 during his "miracle year" of 1665, when he first began formulating the principles that would dominate physics until 1905. That was when Einstein, only 26, experienced his "miracle year."

Newton's religious views were a product of both his era and his temperament. Newton was born on Christmas Day in 1642, the year in which Galileo died. For the last 10 years of his life Galileo had been under a form of house arrest in Italy—eventually in his own home in the hills above Florence. He had been tried in 1633 by the Inquisition of the Roman Catholic church for holding heretical views about the motion of the Earth. His heresy lay in believing in the Copernican theory—the thesis advocated by the Polish astronomer

Copernicus that the Earth moved around the Sun—which appeared to contradict the Bible. At the time, a man could go to prison—or worse—for holding such heretical views in the name of science. In Newton's time, there was more freedom to engage in science, but the idea that science and religion were separate enterprises would have appeared absurd to Newton. For Newton, the Bible was the literal truth and could be used as scientific evidence in the same way as any other kind of scientific observation. Newton spent a great deal of his time studying the Bible to learn when the universe had been created and when it would end. After a lifetime of such study he concluded that the world would not end before the year 2060, a claim that many of the readers of this book may live to verify personally. For Newton, this sort of prediction was also science. His God was present in every activity of the universe, providing the ultimate frame against which to measure the motions in space and in time. He was also a severe God, and Newton a severe man. For a five-year period, when he was at the height of his scientific activity, Newton had an assistant who reported having seen him laugh just once, when someone asked him to describe the practical use of the study of geometry. Newton never married, and indeed the evidence is that he died a virgin. Apart from science, what could he and Einstein have possibly been able to discuss?

Before turning to Einstein's miracle year of 1905, let us bring our biographical story up to date. When we left Einstein in 1900, he had completed his study at the ETH and had passed his final examinations with reasonable if not outstanding grades. He was hoping to find a job as an assistant to one of the professors at the ETH, a post that would have led naturally into the next stage of his career. But none of the professors offered Einstein a job. In fact, Einstein did not get a job until June 1902, when he was hired on a trial basis as a patent examiner third class, or technical expert, at the Swiss National Patent Office in Bern, at an annual salary of 3,500 Swiss francs. (This was not a bad salary considering that one could get a good room with board for about 70 Swiss francs a month.) Prior to his employment, Einstein had been eking out his living by temporary tutorial work and a monthly allowance from his parents, some of which he used to pay the costs of his Swiss citizenship in 1901. Why he had such difficulty getting a job is made clear in a letter Mileva Maric wrote to her friend Helene Savic late in 1901. In it she wrote, "Now the air has cleared to some extent, i.e., Albert's parents are not so terribly angry with him any more. In addition we have the misfortune that Albert has not got a position; he is now in Schaffhausen, where he is employed as a tutor. You can imagine he does not feel good in such a state of dependency. Yet, it is not likely that he will soon get a secure position; you know that my sweetheart has a very wicked tongue and is a Jew into the bargain...."

Einstein at his desk at the patent office in Bern, 1905.

Being a Jew was certainly a handicap, but still worse was the impression Einstein made on the senior professors at the ETH, who might have been able to help him. They saw in him what we might call a wiseguy, a student whose attendance in class was sporadic and whose attitude was not respectful. They had no idea of the immense amount of work Einstein was doing on his own to teach himself the physics he could not learn in class. One gets some sense of this from the reaction of Hermann Minkowski, a brilliant mathematician who had been one of Einstein's teachers at the ETH, when he learned that it was

Einstein who had devised the theory of relativity. In 1908, Minkowski invented the formulation of relativity that is the one still used today, involving the four-dimensional geometry of space and time. When told that it was Einstein who had created the theory, Minkowski could not believe it. He remembered Einstein as being a "lazy dog," probably incapable of doing anything serious.

In October 1902 Hermann Einstein died in Italy, and the following January Albert married Mileva. Earlier in the year he had helped to found the Olympia Academy in Bern. The Academy began and ended with three members: Maurice Solovine, Conrad Habicht, and Einstein. Habicht was studying to become a mathematics teacher. Solovine had encountered Einstein through an advertisement. Einstein had put an ad in a Bern newspaper announcing that he would give private lessons in physics for three francs an hour, and Solovine had answered the ad. At the first lesson Solovine discovered that he and Einstein had a common interest in certain philosophers—especially those who wrote about the philosophy of science. The two decided to meet regularly to discuss philosophy and science, and Habicht joined them. Jokingly, they named their meetings the "Academy," and these continued even after Einstein's marriage. Solovine's descriptions of the meetings, and especially of one on Einstein's birthday, are delightful. Solovine, who was of Romanian origin, had tasted caviar, a rare and expensive delicacy, in his parents' home. He and Habicht decided that on his birthday, Einstein should taste caviar, and they brought him some. But that night Einstein was to lecture to them about the work of Galileo. He became so interested in the subject of his lecture that he ate all the caviar without paying the slightest attention to what he was eating. Caviar or no caviar, both Solovine and Habicht knew from the beginning that Einstein was very special. They were probably the least surprised of anyone by what Einstein created during the "miracle year" of 1905.

The really important role of the Academy was that it focused Einstein's attention on the kind of reasoning that was needed to reexamine the work of Newton. It was not that philosophers like the 18th-century Scottish philosopher David Hume or the 19th-century Austrian physicist-philosopher Ernst Mach—whom the three Academy members studied—had knowledge of specific aspects of physics that Einstein needed. What he needed was their skeptical attitude, and above all Mach's dissatisfaction with the physics of Newton, at least as Newton had formulated it. Mach never claimed that Newton's physics was actually wrong. He was concerned with the way in which Newton expressed it, mixing theology—in which God was the ultimate frame of reference—with science. Mach expressed these doubts in the book *The Science of Mechanics,* which was published in 1883 and frequently discussed by the Olympia Academy.

Some scientists keep diaries so that they can record their progress, or lack of it, on a daily basis. Since Einstein apparently did not keep a diary, one has to try to reconstruct the steps that led to the theory of relativity from various fragments. Some of these fragments involve personal memories that he recalled and described long after the founding of the theory. Others involve letters written at the time—some of which do not entirely agree with these memories. The result makes it difficult to really understand how Einstein created the theory of relativity. But that often seems to be the case with the "creative leap" that accompanies any great act of artistic or scientific creation. Had I been able to meet Einstein, knowing what I now know, I would have liked to have asked him dozens of questions about all of this, but I am not sure that even after hearing his answers I would have understood his creative process all that much better.

In his biography of Einstein, Philipp Frank provides an account of how Einstein arrived at the theory of relativity that he must have heard from Einstein himself since Einstein also provides it in his "autobiography." According to Frank's account, Einstein began asking himself some of the key questions leading up to relativity when he was 16 and a high school student in Aarau. These questions revolved around a "thought experiment." Thought experiments are physics experiments that we perform in our imaginations, since they are beyond our ability to perform in the laboratory. Sometimes it turns out that experiments that were thought experiments for one generation of physicists become real experiments for a future generation, since experimental techniques are constantly improving. Such was the case in this instance.

Einstein's thought experiment was to imagine what the world would look like if he or any other material object were able to travel at the speed of light, or even faster. Ten years earlier, in 1886, Ernst Mach had actually performed experiments with projectiles—objects that are propelled by an external force—that moved faster than the speed of sound. These led to the "Mach numbers," which describe the speed of an object: An object moving with the speed of sound in air has attained "Mach 1," and objects moving faster than this have attained Mach numbers greater than 1. From the viewpoint of Newtonian physics there was no reason in principle why a projectile, or any other object, could not be made to move at any speed, however great, whether the speed of light or the speed of sound. One would only have to continually supply the necessary force to keep accelerating the object. That was Einstein's idea: to imagine that he himself could keep accelerating until he reached the speed of light.

In the spirit of Einstein's "experiment," imagine that you are on a railroad train that is moving along an ideal set of tracks so that there is no bumping or jarring. Let us suppose that you are rich enough to have an entire private compartment to yourself, with a washbasin in it. It is dark, but you decide to comb your hair. There is a light behind your head and a mirror a couple of feet from you. When you switch the light on, the light will travel to the mirror and then be reflected back into your eyes, so that you can see your face. It will take only an instant to do so, because the speed of light is so great. This speed, which is usually designated by the letter c, is 299,792,458 meters per second. (It is convenient to rewrite this as 2.99792×10^8, where $10^8 = 100,000,000$.) The quantity c is the speed of light in a vacuum. That light is able to travel in a complete vacuum is a remarkable circumstance and contrasts with the way sound propagates. Sound propagation involves the vibration of the molecules of a medium, such as those on the surface of a drum or the air. Sound will not propagate in a vacuum. When light travels in a medium like air or water, it is slowed down by collisions with atoms in these media. But even when this medium is evacuated, light will still propagate.

Returning to our thought experiment, let us suppose that just before you got up to comb your hair, the engineer had revved the engines of the train so that it was now moving along the rails at the speed of light, c. You now switch on your light. Will you still see your face in the mirror? This is one of the questions that Einstein asked himself in his thought experiment. To put the matter in context, the generally held view among physicists at the time Einstein began asking these questions was that the transmission of light and sound were similar, in that both required the presence of a medium that would carry them from place to place. However, it was clear that light propagated from the stars to the Earth in what appears to be a vacuum. But because the idea of light waves traveling through a vacuum was unacceptable to these physicists, they invented a medium that filled all space. They called this medium the "ether." Thus, for example, the striking of a match was considered to create vibrations in the ether that then travelled outward through it like the vibrations produced by striking a drum with a stick. Such vibrations move away from their source with a speed that depends on the properties of the medium through which they are travelling. In the case of sound, for example, the more dense the medium, the slower the speed at which the sound travels. Once such a wave is generated, there is no reason why we cannot—at least according to classical Newtonian physics—run alongside it or even pass it. The pre-Einsteinian physicists of Mach's time would have claimed that this was as true of light as it was of sound. Returning to the case of our train, such a physicist would have predicted that if the train was traveling exactly at the speed of light through the ether, the light from the bulb behind your face would not be able to catch up with the mirror, and you would not be able to see your face. This bothered Einstein, but at the time it did not seem to bother anyone else.

Our thought experiment with the mirror on the train does not depend in its analysis on whether light behaves like a wave or particle. In either case we can catch up to and run past the light and not see our face. However, Einstein's second thought experiment involved the wave nature of light. Below is a very simple wave.

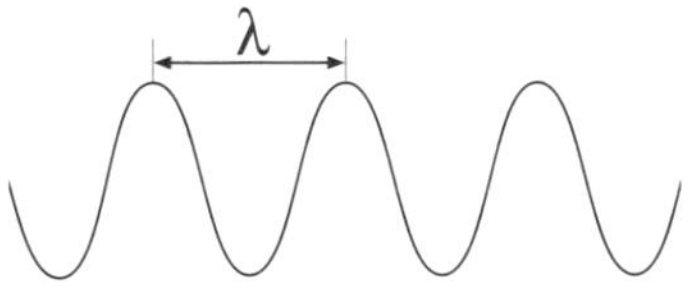

Figure 5

The thing to note about the wave is that the pattern repeats itself periodically. If we pick one of the high points along the path of the wave and measure the distance to the next high point, this distance is known as the "wave length," and is usually denoted by the Greek letter lambda: λ. If it takes a time T for the wave to travel one wave length, or from one high point to the next, then the speed of propagation of the wave is λ/T. That is because speed equals distance divided by time, or:

Speed = Distance/Time

Suppose that I now decide to run alongside the wave. If I do so at the speed of propagation of the wave, I can keep

text continues on page 52

A SHORT HISTORY OF LIGHT THEORY

In the second half of the 17th century, the two dominant theorists in physics were Isaac Newton and the somewhat older Dutch physicist and astronomer Christian Huygens. Huygens believed that light propagated as a wave, pure and simple. When two such waves meet they produce a resultant wave whose properties are derived from the two interacting waves. Where each of the intersecting waves has a large height, the resultant wave will have an even larger height. On the other hand, if the trough of one wave overlaps the crest of the other, the two waves can cancel each other out at the places in which this happens—a phenomenon known as *destructive interference.* We can observe such phenomena by dropping pebbles into a pond and watching how the waves collide with one another and change each others' shape as they pass through each other. Huygens proposed to explain the observed properties of light, such as the bending of light in a medium like water (known as "refraction") on the basis of such effects occurring with light waves.

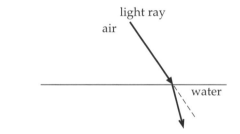

Figure 6

Newton's views of light were more complex. Newton was an "atomist." In his book on light, called *Opticks,* he wrote that "It seems probable to me, that God in the Beginning form'd Matter in solid, massy, hard impenetrable moveable particles...even so hard, as never to wear out or break in pieces; no ordinary Power being able to divide what God himself made one in the first Creation." It would then have been natural for Newton to think of light as also being made up of particles. However, there were certain phenomena that seemed to make such a particle theory of light difficult to maintain. Newton himself studied one of them—the so-called Newton's rings, or rainbow-like rings that show up in soap bubbles or patches of oil on the sidewalk. It was

continues on page 50

continued from page 49

quite unclear how the propagation of particles could explain such phenomena, and, indeed, in his *Opticks* Newton referred to patterns of reflection and refraction, a concept that sounds very much like wave propagation. However, he also recognized that light travels in straight lines, which resembles the manner in which particles would travel. Hence, Newton appeared to be saying that light seemed to have characteristics of both waves and particles—something that, as we shall see, became the centerpiece of Einstein's other 1905 discovery that light was a particle as well as a wave.

Newton's followers did not appreciate these fine distinctions, and maintained a strict particle theory of light. Hence, in the beginning of the 19th century there were wave theorists and particle theorists standing in opposition to each other. Soon thereafter, however, the matter appeared to have been settled definitively in favor of the wave theory. The first experiments that strengthened this theory were the work of the British genius Thomas Young. Young, born in 1773, learned to read when he was two, and by the time he was six had read the Bible through twice and had begun the study of Latin. In later life he made important contributions toward deciphering Egyptian hieroglyphics. In 1800 Young published his first paper on the nature of light. It was he who first maintained that light waves combine by "superimposing" on one another to produce a resultant wave. Huygens, in contrast, had maintained that this was true only in limited cases. Young applied these ideas to one of the most famous series of experiments ever done in physics. They involved the phenomenon called "diffraction."

To demonstrate diffraction, we can make two holes a few millimeters apart in a screen and let light from a distant source shine on the screen.

If we then put a second target screen behind the first, so that it can be illuminated by the light passing through the holes,

Figure 7

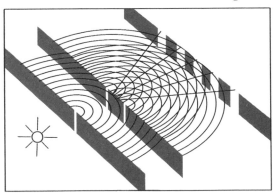

two patches of light will appear on the target screen when the holes in the first screen are large. When the holes in the first screen are made smaller, we naturally expect their images on the target screen to grow smaller as well. By assuming that light particles travel in straight lines, we can predict how much smaller the patches of light on the target screen should become. At first this works as expected, but Young showed that when the holes in the first screen are made small enough, the patches of light on the target screen actually become *larger!*

This result seems to be completely incomprehensible according to the concept of light as a phenomenon involving particles traveling in straight lines, which would produce light patches of the same size as the holes in the first screen. In order for the patch of light to grow larger, it means that in some sense part of the light must "go around a corner" as it passes through the hole in the first screen, something possible for a wave but seemingly impossible for particles constrained to move in straight lines. What is still more incomprehensible according to the particle concept is what happens if the two holes are made even smaller. The patches of light will then overlap and be crossed by fine dark bands. Young explained these results as being caused by the interference of light waves with each other.

Young's work was followed by even more precise experimentation done by the French physicist Augustin-Jean Fresnel. By the time Einstein was introduced to these ideas there was no doubt in anyone's mind that light was a wave phenomenon. Indeed, in 1868, James Clerk Maxwell published a paper entitled "Note on the Electromagnetic Theory of Light," in which he demonstrated that light was an electromagnetic wave—a combination of an electrical force and a magnetic force—that varies periodically in strength. Maxwell considered these electromagnetic waves as oscillating—or traveling with a forward as well as up-and-down motion—in the ether. It was this picture of light that Einstein had in mind in 1896 when he was in high school in Aarau.

pace with one of the high points, or maxima, of the wave, or with one of the low points, or with any point in between these two points. But if I do that, the wave will no longer look to me like a wave. It will merely seem like a disturbance of some fixed magnitude and I will never observe the wave properties since nothing goes by me periodically. When this happens I know that I am traveling at the speed of the wave, just as in the mirror example you knew that you were traveling at the speed of light when you could no longer see your face. Why did this bother Einstein? Fifty years after conceiving the theory of relativity, Einstein, in his autobiography, remembered the wave example and referred to it as a "paradox"—a statement that seems to contradict itself. It is in this paradox that we shall first meet relativity.

The idea of relativity in physics, although it did not yet go by that name, has a history going back to Galileo in the 17th century. One of the objections that Galileo had to confront when he defended the Copernican theory was that if the Earth really moved, why didn't the birds get left behind every time they flew off the ground? To counter this argument, Galileo claimed to have done the following experiment. He was then living in Venice, a place where boats were common since it is a seaport. Galileo said that he had dropped weights from the mast of a smoothly moving sailing ship. He could then see whether these weights fell to the base of the mast or were left behind as the ship moved, as the opponents of the Copernican theory were claiming. He later wrote that he had observed the weights land at the base of the mast, a result of which he was sure, even before he did the experiment. Why was he so sure? We know from our experience that if a vehicle is moving at a constant speed, we can conduct all of our activities in it just as if it were at rest. Indeed, for all practical purposes we can think of our vehicle as being at rest and the ground moving underneath it. In the case of Galileo's ship experiment, we can think of the ship as being at rest and the sea moving uniformly under it. Hence, looked at this way, it is not surprising that the weights dropped from the mast land at its foot, just as they would if the ship were not moving. The word "relativity" enters here because it is only the relative motion of the ship and the ocean that has any meaning. We can consider the ship at rest and the ocean moving, or the ocean at rest and the ship moving. The two situations are perfectly equivalent. It is only the relative motion of the one with respect to the other that matters. If we go down in the ship's hold and don't look out the porthole, we can never tell whether we are moving at all, so long as there are no accelerations—that is, so long as we are moving with a constant speed. We might be at rest in the ocean or moving along smoothly. Down in the hold we cannot tell the difference.

Now we begin to get a glimmer of what was bothering Einstein. This relativity principle—called the Galilean relativity principle after Galileo—is built into Newton's theory of motion. This is the theory in which forces produce accelerations according to Newton's famous law $F = ma$, where F is the force, m the mass of the object being accelerated, and a the acceleration. One consequence of this law is that for forces like that of gravity, one cannot distinguish between an object at rest and an object moving uniformly by making experiments involving things like throwing balls or dropping objects. Returning to the case of our railway car, I can set up a billiard table in my compartment and play a game of billiards—and never know that the train is moving unless it accelerates (speeds up) or decelerates (slows down). In particular, I cannot devise a mechanical experiment done inside my compartment with the shades down that will enable me to tell how fast I am going with respect to the tracks. From the viewpoint of relativity, the train is not moving at all. It is the tracks that are moving.

But what about experiments with light? Of course real trains cannot travel at the speed of light. But in Einstein's thought experiment they can. We can now perform Einstein's thought experiment with light. But lo and behold it appears to violate the relativity principle! If I don't see my face in the mirror I can say that I am moving at the speed of light. I don't have to look out the window at the tracks. I can keep the shades down and determine my speed. This, Einstein recalls, bothered him terribly. In his autobiography he writes, "One sees in this paradox the germ of the special theory of relativity."

We can put the situation this way. Newton's mechanics allows us to move with the speed of light. But if we could move with the speed of light we could construct an experiment with light, at least in a thought experiment, that violates the principle of relativity. Hence we cannot have both Newtonian mechanics and the principle of relativity. Something has to give. Einstein claims to have understood the essentials of this dilemma when he was 16. Moreover, he claims that it was "intuitively clear" to him that it was the principle of relativity that was right. He believed that Newtonian mechanics, which had stood unchallenged for two centuries, had to be wrong! One would think that having had such a radical set of ideas, Einstein would have tried to tell them to anyone who would listen. In fact, there was at least one person who was only too eager to listen, and that was Einstein's mother's brother, Caesar Koch. This uncle seems to have taken a special interest in Einstein. At the time we are discussing, the summer of 1895, Einstein sent his uncle a letter in which he seems to have enclosed a document that reads like a research proposal. It has to do with investigating the properties of the ether. In this document Einstein describes light as if it were propagating in an elastic medium, such as air, like a sound wave. It is a document that could have been written by any conventional 19th-century physicist. There is not a single word in it about the paradox that relativity, as it applies to the speed of light, introduces into Newtonian mechanics. This is very puzzling, since it was just at this time that Einstein later claimed to have begun to have doubts about the ether theory—the paradoxes we discussed earlier.

Another mystery connected with the creation of relativity revolves around the question of what Einstein knew. He was not the only person thinking about these matters at the time. What did he know about this other work? The most important piece of work of which he might have known is what is called the Michelson–Morley experiment, which is one of the most celebrated experiments in the history of physics. In this experiment, performed in 1887 by the American physicist Albert Michelson and assisted by the chemist Edward Morley, was an attempt to measure the effect on the speed of light by the Earth's motion through the ether. It was a very sophisticated version of Einstein's thought experiment about trying to see one's self in the mirror on a rapidly moving train—although, of course, Michelson and Morley had never heard of Einstein, who was then eight years old.

On the other hand, how much did Einstein know of the Michelson–Morley experiment? That is still a matter of argument among historians of science. Einstein is of some help here, but not much. At various times he said that he had either heard of Michelson's work, or that he hadn't, or that if

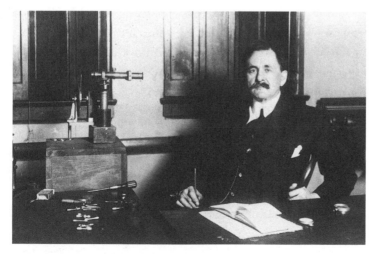

In 1887 the American physicist Albert Michelson (left), assisted by chemist Edward Morley, conducted a sophisticated experiment to measure the effect on the speed of light by the Earth's motion in space. Michelson's conclusions contributed to Einstein's theory of relativity.

he had heard of it, it didn't matter. In any case, there is no reference to any of this work in Einstein's 1905 paper on the theory of relativity. In a letter Einstein wrote shortly before his death, he said, "In my own development Michelson's result has not had a considerable influence." Why?

For the purposes of the Michelson–Morley experiment, we can consider the Earth to be moving uniformly. We are not aware that the Earth is moving around the Sun at a rate of 30 kilometers per second. Hence, from our viewpoint the Michelson apparatus is at rest. But if we believe in the principle of relativity, a Michelson experiment or any other cannot possibly detect the effects of such a uniform motion through the ether; it can only give an experimental argument in favor of the principle of relativity. But since Einstein was sure the principle was right anyway, he did not need such an argument. For him the real problems lay elsewhere.

If Einstein was aware of the paradoxes that led to the theory of relativity when he was 16, why did he not create the theory until 10 years later? The answer is that it took him 10 years to reanalyze the nature of time.

If we think about it, we realize that there are two kinds of time. There is "subjective time," which involves things such as our sense of aging, and there is what we might call "objective time," which is something that is measured by clocks. The two are connected, since we can date or order a series of events by referring to clocks. That we can communicate with each other about such things means that at least to some degree, we all have a common sense of time. This common sense of time can be elevated to a principle of "absolute time," a principle that was first clearly enunciated by Newton. In the *Principia,* he wrote that "Absolute, true, and mathematical time, of itself, and from its own nature, flows equably without relation to anything external, and by another name is called duration." As obscure as this definition of absolute time may seem, it does have consequences, and one of them is to make it possible, according to Newtonian physics, for a person to catch up with a light wave.

To understand this, let us consider Figure 8.

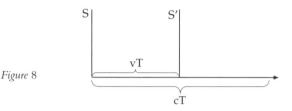

Figure 8

To see why a physicist before Einstein's era would claim that it was possible to catch up with a light wave, we can examine Figure 8. There is an observer at rest who we will call S. This observer sends out a light wave. According to this observer, the wave travels a distance cT in the time T. But we also have a moving observer—that is, an observer whom S sees in motion. Let us call this observer S'. During the time T, this observer moves to the right a distance vT. Hence, according to this observer, the light would only have to go a distance of cT - vT = T(c-v) to reach the same point. To this moving observer, according to a pre-Einsteinian physicist, the speed of light would be only c-v. If this observer moved with the speed c, he or she could catch up to the light beam. If in the expression c-v, you put in v=c then you get zero, which means that you have caught up with the light. However, an assumption has been "slipped in" here. The assumption is that both observers would agree on what is meant by the time T. If this assumption is given up, we can no longer conclude that an observer moving at speed c could catch up with the light wave. The speeds may not add up the way Newton claimed they did. Einstein did give up this assumption, and we must examine with care his reasoning in doing so.

Since Einstein did not keep a diary of his work, we do not know the daily or yearly progress he made toward the theory of relativity. His letters to Mileva give occasional hints that he is working on something, but most of the references also include references to the ether, which would disappear from Einstein's thinking after 1905. It seems as if the final formulation of the theory of relativity came to Einstein very rapidly in the spring of 1905. His paper about it was written in June, and it is likely that he did not have the theory clearly in mind until five or six weeks earlier.

Einstein dated the time of his final inspiration to a visit he made to his friend Michele Besso that spring. Besso had been working in the patent office in Bern since 1904, and the two men and their families saw a great deal of each other. Einstein later recalled that he went over to Besso's house to try out a few ideas on Besso, who was an excellent sounding board. Suddenly in the middle of this, Einstein understood everything. Time depends on velocity!

The essential thing in Einstein's realization was that a precise notion of time was linked to a precise notion of simultaneity. Early in his 1905 paper he wrote, "We have to take into account that all our judgments in which time plays a role are always judgments of *simultaneous events*. If, for instance, I say, 'That train arrives here at 7 o'clock,' I mean something like this: 'The pointing of the small hand of my watch to 7 and the arrival of the train are simultaneous events.'"

If two events happen at the same location in space, we have an intuitive understanding of what it means for them to be simultaneous. The difficulty arises if we ask what it means for two events to be simultaneous if they happen at points distant from each other. How in such a case, do we know that these events happened simultaneously? If the speed of light were infinite rather than merely very large, we would have no problem, since we could "see" the events as they happened and compare our observation with the reading of any clock near us. Newton and his successors had implicitly assumed that the speed of light was infinite, and therefore never carefully considered this matter. To understand the issues it brings up, let us consider an example of which Einstein was fond, involving a train moving uniformly along a track. Here we will call S' the observer on the train and S the observer anchored to the track. Now we imagine that two lightning bolts strike the track at points that are equidistant from a central observer.

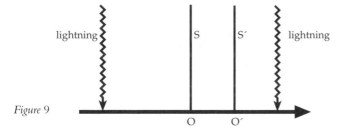

Figure 9

What does it mean for these two lightning bolts to have struck their respective points *simultaneously?* We can imagine the following arrangement. We have observers stationed beside the track, and when one of them records the arrival of a lightning bolt, he or she instantly sends a light signal to the observer at the central point O in Figure 9. If two such signals arrive at O at the same time, we can conclude that the lightning struck simultaneously at the points where the two observers are stationed. We can, in fact, take this as the definition of what we mean by the simultaneous occurrence of two distant events. So far so good.

But what will the individual located at O', the origin of the coordinates in S', observe? Here we must take into account the motion of the observer at O' relative to the observer anchored in the system S. The observer at O' is moving toward the light coming from the right and away from the light coming from the left. Therefore the distances over which these two light beams travel before reaching O' are different. The beam coming from the right travels a shorter distance in reaching O' than does the one coming from the left. Hence the two light beams will not arrive at O' at the same time. The observer at O' will be obliged to conclude—not being able to "see" the lightning bolts that have struck perhaps miles away—that they did not strike simultaneously. In fact, the observer at O' will conclude, quite reasonably, that the lightning bolt that struck to the right did so earlier than the one that struck to the left. Consequently, the observer at O and the observer at O′ will disagree about the times to assign to these lightning strikes. The observer at O might say they both occurred at noon, while the second observer would say that according to his or her clocks, the bolt to the left struck at one second after noon while the one on the right struck at one second before noon. Who is right?

In this case, both observers are right. How the clocks read depends on whether you are talking about the system at S or the system at S′. While a Newtonian could have made the same set of arguments, none did, although a few of Einstein's predecessors did make vague remarks about re-thinking the nature of time. A Newtonian who followed this line of argument could even invoke another reason why the lightning bolts arrived at O′ at different times. When the train moves toward the beam of light being sent from the lightning strike on the right, such an individual would call the speed of light c+v, but would call it c−v when the train is moving away. But with our new analysis of time we are not obliged to assume that the velocities of a light wave and a moving object add up in this way. For constant velocities, $v′= x′/T′$. However, we now know that T and T′ are not the same, and we therefore cannot write that $v′= x′/T$. Velocities may differ according to differences in time. The time intervals are not the same for resting and moving observers and this will affect the velocities.

At this point, Einstein made an assumption that was much more daring than the relativity principle. He assumed that the speed of light in S and S′ was the same. It does not matter whether you are moving toward or away from the light beam, the sum of its velocity and your velocity will always be the same. We must take a moment to digest this. It is a very radical idea. To put things graphically, suppose you are in a spaceship heading toward a star at half the speed of the light coming from the star. How fast is the light from the star moving toward you? The answer is c! If you now speed up your spaceship to three quarters of the speed of light, the answer is still c. This is what Einstein called the "principle of constancy." We cannot object that this principle violates our rule about adding up velocities because that rule assumed that time was absolute: that T = T'. But since we know that T and T' are not the same, new rules such as the constancy of the speed of light may apply.

When Einstein enunciated the principle of constancy in his paper on relativity, there was no direct experimental evidence for it. It was—although no one had paid attention to this—a feature of Maxwell's theory of electromagnetism. Whenever Maxwell's theory and Newton's theory disagreed, Einstein chose Maxwell.

What we have seen so far should convince you that it is not crazy to think of time as a function of velocity. But just how does time depend on velocity? In his paper, Einstein analyzes this without reference to any particular kind of clock. For the purpose of his argument a clock is any physical system that shows periodic behavior. It can be the swinging back and forth of a pendulum or the vibration of an atom. Let us consider a specific kind of clock whose workings are easy to analyze. This is more a "thought" clock than a real clock.

Suppose we take two mirrors and set them up as shown in Figure 10 below.

If the distance between the mirrors is L, then it takes a time T = 2L/c for the light clock to make one round trip from one mirror to the other and back again. This is the natural period of the light clock at rest. One "tick" of the clock is 2L/c. But suppose I now set the "clock" in motion to the right, with the speed v. Below is a figure that shows how

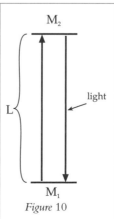

Figure 10

the path of the light now looks to an observer in S—the "rest system."

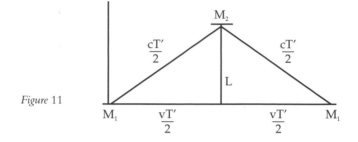

Figure 11

In this system we see that the path of light from and back to the clock is triangular. I have indicated on the figure the lengths of the sides of the triangles that enter into our discussion. I have called T' the period of the moving clock as measured by the observer at rest in S. We don't yet know what T' is, but during this time T' the clock will have moved a distance vT' to the right. This explains the lengths assigned to the bases of the triangles. In assigning the length L to the altitude of the triangle, we have assumed that if the motion of the light clock is to have any effect on the length of the side of any triangle, it will have such an effect only in the direction of the motion. Lengths at right angles to the motion will not be affected. This seems reasonable, but it can only be tested when we derive the relevant formulas and test them with experiments. A length cT'/2 has been assigned to the hypotenuse of the triangle whose other sides are vT'/2 and L. In doing this I have invoked the principle of constancy, maintaining that the velocity of light, c, has the same value to all observers. We can now use the Pythagorean theorem as follows to relate these quantities.

$$\frac{c^2T'^2}{4} = L^2 + \frac{v^2T'^2}{4}$$

If we solve the foregoing expression for T', we get

$$T' = 2\frac{L}{C} \times \frac{1}{\sqrt{1-v^2/c^2}} = \frac{T}{\sqrt{1-v^2/c^2}}$$

where, as before, T=2L/c. At this point it is useful to do a little investigation of the factor $1/\sqrt{(1-(v/c)^2)}$.

If we put in a few numerical values of v/c, such as half the velocity of light or nine-tenths the velocity of light, and evaluate one divided by the square root of this, we find that the result is always greater than one. In other words, T′ is always greater than T. As the speed v approaches c, the difference between T and T′ becomes ever greater. This is something that physicists call "time dilatation." Moving clocks are slower than identical clocks at rest. It is in this sense that time is a function of velocity.

This is such a bizarre notion that it is important to clear up some common misconceptions about it. The first is that S′ need not be considered the moving system or observer. An observer in S′ has a perfect right to claim that he or she is at rest and that the observer S is moving backwards. The S′ observer could then go through the same argument with the triangles and conclude that the S clocks run slow. As is usual in relativity, the relative motion is the only thing that matters. A clock that is moving relative to me will lag, and a clock that is moving relative to you will also lag. That is what Einstein predicts. A second misconception is that this lag has something to do with the actual mechanism of the clock. Perhaps somehow by moving the clock we have jiggled it, so that it now runs slow. But if we tie a clock to a post and run past it, we can legitimately consider ourselves to be at rest and the clock to be moving. As far as we are concerned, the clock in this case will also run slow compared to any clocks we are carrying. The great difference between Einstein and his predecessors is that they were looking for mechanisms to explain effects such as this, while Einstein was pointing out that such effects have to do with how we measure time and not with any special mechanism.

When Einstein drew these conclusions about the nature of time in his 1905 paper, there was no way to test them directly. However, he did propose an experiment of sorts, which he may have meant more as a joke than a real experiment. He recommended taking two identical clocks and putting one at the North Pole and the other at the equator. The clock at the North Pole is at rest, since the Earth is turning around this point. But the clock at the equator is in motion. If we take the circumference of the Earth and divide it by the number of seconds in a day—the time it takes for the earth to rotate once—the speed of the equator relative to the North Pole is about 0.46 meters per second. This is minuscule compared to the speed of light. In fact, if we apply Einstein's formula, we learn that the equatorial clock is predicted to lag the Polar clock by about one ten-millionths of a second a day!

But what would have happened in 1905 if some superb Swiss watchmaker had been able to make watches accurate enough for this experiment? Einstein would have been in for a surprise. Instead of showing this time lag, the experiment would have shown no time lag at all. Does this mean that one has to throw the theory of relativity out the window? Not really. What Einstein did not know in 1905 (he discovered it a few years later) was that gravity also affects clocks. In this case the special relativity effect and the gravity effect exactly cancel one another. This was tested in the 1970s by flying incredibly accurate atomic clocks in airplanes from one latitude to another. The tests confirmed the predictions of both the special relativity theory and the gravity effect.

Long before this, however, the concept of time dilation had been directly tested in experiments done with very rapidly moving particles created in particle accelerators or arriving from outer space in the form of cosmic rays. Most of these particles are unstable and decay into other particles. This takes a certain amount of time, which is known as the mean life of the particle. It is usually very short, and is measured in microseconds or less. Because the mean lives of particles constitute a kind of clock, we should expect to observe a difference between the mean life of a particle at rest and the mean life of the same particle in rapid motion—and indeed, differences at different particle speeds. The effect has been observed countless times in high-energy physics laboratories by studying the tracks that these particles leave in detectors. The tracks are much longer than they would be if the particles did not have their lives extended by being in motion. My teacher, Philipp Frank, once commented on the slowing of time in relativity by saying, "Travel and stay young."

In the next chapter I will describe how these ideas, and the others that Einstein created in 1905, were received by his fellow scientists. It is an interesting story. But I would like to finish this chapter by telling you an anecdote that Helen Dukas, Einstein's secretary at Princeton, once told me. In 1943 Einstein was asked to help the Allies' effort in World War II by auctioning off the manuscript of his relativity paper. Unfortunately, he had never saved the original manuscript. But he had an idea. If Miss Dukas would read him the paper he would copy it down, and this copy, in his own handwriting, could be sold. It was sold to an insurance company for $5 million worth of war bonds and then placed in the Library of Congress in Washington. At one point, while Miss Dukas was reading the paper to Einstein, he stopped her and asked if that was what he had really written. When assured that it was, he remarked that he now realized that he could have said it much more simply.

In 1943, a handwritten copy of Einstein's paper on relativity was sold to an insurance company for $5 million worth of war bonds.

Einstein with his first wife, Mileva, and their son Hans Albert, 1904.

The Strange Story of the Quantum

As we saw in the last chapter, Einstein and Mileva were married in January 1903. There is every reason to believe that the marriage began as a happy one and that the couple welcomed the birth of their first son, whom they named Hans Albert, in May 1904. In September of that year Einstein's appointment at the Swiss patent office was upgraded to a permanent position. Einstein did so much fundamental work in physics during this period—writing five superb papers and his Ph.D. thesis in 1905 alone—that it is tempting to think that his job in the patent office was not very time-consuming. But this was not the case.

He took the job of examining applications for patents for inventions very seriously. He enjoyed the work: he liked inventions and inventors. In the late 1920s he even took out several patents himself, registered jointly with the Hungarian physicist Leo Szilard. One of them was for a noiseless refrigerator. It would have worked, but easier methods were found. But around 1905, when Einstein was creating modern physics, he was managing a household with a young son and working full-time in an office. The physics was done in his spare time.

We have seen how Einstein's 1905 paper on relativity changed our notions of space and time. Now let us see how it changed our notion of mass. A good place to begin this discussion is with Newton's fundamental law of motion, F = ma (Force equals mass times acceleration), which we saw earlier but did not really discuss. Newton's great insight was that the role of a force is to *change* the motion of an object. An object on which no force acts will either remain at rest or continue to move at a constant speed. This was an idea that was very difficult for Newton's predecessors to accept—at least as difficult in its day as the idea that time depends on velocity is in ours. The reason for this was that we never find in practice any physical system on which no forces act. If, for example, we roll a ball, it will sooner or later come to a stop. We explain this by saying that the force of friction has acted on the ball, causing it to decelerate, or slow down. There is no situation in our common experience in which some friction does not exist. Surfaces such as ice may exhibit less friction than others such as concrete or wood, but it takes a leap of the imagination to assume that in the absence of any force a ball would continue to roll on forever, as is predicted by Newton's law.

There are three quantities in Newton's law—force, F; acceleration, a; and mass, m. But Newton's mechanics does not tell us what the force, F, is. That is something we have to find out by experimentation. We have to see in a given situation whether it is an electrical force, a gravitational force, or some other kind of force that is producing the acceleration. Newton's law tells us only that when we apply such a force to an object, the object will accelerate—its velocity will change. But it is a common part of our experience that bodies respond differently to the same force: a soccer ball will go a lot farther than the Empire State Building if you kick the two of them with the same force! We say that this happens because the Empire State Building is vastly more "massive" than a soccer ball. If we take a standard object, any object will do, we can measure the mass of another object by comparing how the two objects accelerate when the same force acts on them. Mass measured in this way is best referred to as the "inertial mass" of an object, since it is a measure of the magnitude of an object's resistance to being accelerated when a known, measured force acts on it.

If we assume that relativity is right, Newton's law in the form expressed above, F = ma, must certainly be wrong. The reason for this is simple: Newton's law predicts that an object to which a constant force is applied will continue to accelerate. It will go faster and faster, and there is nothing in Newton's law that says we cannot eventually make it go faster than the speed of light. But relativity does not allow us to do this; we cannot have both Newton's law—at least in the form stated by Newton—and relativity. Something must change. It turns out, as Einstein also showed in his 1905 paper—that what changes is the *notion* of mass. In Newton's law, the mass of an object does not depend on the velocity at which it is traveling; the mass of the object is the same whether we measure it at rest or in motion. By contrast, in Einstein's law of motion under the theory of relativity, the mass of an object does depend on its velocity. For this reason the mass of an object at rest—its rest mass—is usually denoted by a special symbol, m_o, while the mass of the same object in motion is denoted by the symbol m. In terms of the rest mass of an object, its moving mass, m, is:

$$m = \frac{m_o}{\sqrt{1-v^2/c^2}}$$

Notice that as the velocity v approaches c (where c is the speed of light in a vacuum), the denominator gets smaller and smaller, and hence the mass m gets bigger and bigger. That is, the object becomes harder and harder to accelerate. This is just what we might expect from the theory of relativity: it means that we cannot accelerate a massive object to the speed of light. The force required to do so gets bigger and bigger, finally approaching infinity.

This was surprising enough, but the real shocker in terms of the effect of relativity on mass was contained in a three-page paper that Einstein published in the fall of 1905. It has the somewhat cumbersome title, "Does the Inertia of a Body Depend on its Energy Content?" It was in this paper that Einstein derived the famous equation $E = m_o c^2$, an equation that has not only come to symbolize Einstein, but the entire nuclear age. It is therefore important to examine its origins. Although the relationship $E = m_o c^2$ was contained in Einstein's first paper on relativity, he had not drawn any special attention to it at that time.

The first thing to note about $E = m_o c^2$ is that it predicts that a *huge* amount of energy is contained in any particle of matter, if only we can figure out how to liberate it. To get an idea of how huge this energy is, let us suppose that we could liberate all of the mass in one gram of matter. A gram is not very much matter. A kilogram—a thousand grams— weighs only a little over two pounds. But because the speed of light is so huge, and because it is squared in Einstein's formula, the corresponding energy is enormous. The energy equivalent to one gram of matter could keep a hundred million light bulbs lit for an hour! In practice we do not know any way of liberating the energy in any particular gram of matter that we may happen to have sitting around the house. The most efficient way in which we could do this would be to come across a gram of *antimatter* (matter that resembles ordinary matter except that all its electrical charges are reversed) and let it meet our gram of matter. When they meet they would explode into radiation, which would carry off all the rest-mass energy (that is, $2m_o c^2$) of both the matter and the antimatter. Unfortunately (or fortunately!), there is not very much antimatter in the universe. We have to manufacture it in high-energy particle accelerators. This is done all the time in laboratories that study particle physics, although in minuscule amounts. These laboratories routinely test Einstein's prediction.

In 1905, when Einstein created the theory of relativity, antimatter was completely unknown. It was not discovered until the early 1930s. More significantly, radioactivity had been discovered only nine years earlier by the French physicist Henri Becquerel. People must have realized that radioactivity represented a new source of energy, and they were very puzzled as to where this energy came from. But not until Einstein did anyone explain it. In terms of Einstein's formula the explanation is very simple. The final radioactive decay products of a fixed quantity of matter must have less mass than whatever it is that is decaying. This difference in mass determines how much energy can be released in the radioactive decay. Einstein uses an example of such radioactive decay in his paper. But at the time, so little was known about radioactivity that he was not entirely sure of his explanation. He states only that with such examples his theory "may successfully be put to the test." It is in fact put successfully to the test every time a radioactive atom decays.

One of the fascinating things about Einstein's relativity paper, and about the others that he published during the miracle year of 1905, is how they were received. We must keep in mind that at the time, Einstein, although he had published a few papers in physics, was almost totally unknown. He had no job in a university. In fact, he did not even have a Ph.D. And he was very young—only 26. It is little wonder that his paper on relativity at first made almost no impression at all. This disappointed Einstein, who had assumed, as young people often do, that since he had presented something unconventional there would be an explosive reaction to it. But that would not happen until later.

The fact that it took so long for his paper to be widely understood was at least partly due to the way in which it was written. Einstein made almost no attempt to connect his work to any of the work previously done by other people. His relativity paper does not contain a single reference to another physics paper! The only person acknowledged in his relativity paper was his friend Michele Besso, about whom he said, in concluding the paper, that "in working at the problem here dealt with I have had the loyal assistance of my friend and colleague M. Besso, and that I am indebted to him for several valuable suggestions."

A paper like this would almost certainly not be acceptable to a modern physics journal. Such a journal has referees—professionals working in the field who read the papers that are submitted to the journal. Even a Nobel Prize winner, let alone an unknown 26-year-old, would have to have any such paper reviewed by referees. And one of the things referees look out for is whether a paper contains the necessary references to other people's work. In Einstein's case a referee would very probably have insisted that Einstein cite the work of other people such as Michelson and Morley. As it happened, Einstein sent his paper to the German journal *Annalen der Physik* (Annals of Physics), which was at the time the most prestigious physics journal in Europe and probably in the world. Published in Berlin, it did not really have a refereeing system, only a board of editors. However, if someone had already published in the *Annalen*—which Einstein had— that person's future papers were usually published without being refereed. This is why Einstein could get away with a sentence like "The introduction of a 'luminiferous ether' will prove to be superfluous because the view here to be developed will [not] introduce an 'absolutely resting space' provided with special properties...." Suppose that you were the referee of Einstein's paper and had spent your life working on the "beloved ether," and were now being told by an unknown 26-year-old that your life's work was "superfluous." How would you have felt? Wouldn't you have insisted that Einstein amplify this sentence, adding all sorts of references to the ether (which we now know to be of no interest whatever)? As it stands, Einstein's paper is so perfectly constructed that even today, 90 years after it was written, one can read it to learn how relativity works. It is as fresh a document as on the day it was written: a masterpiece.

The first reference made in a physics journal to Einstein's paper on relativity seems to have appeared in the fall of 1905, in a paper written by the German experimental physicist Walter Kaufmann. For several years Kaufmann had been studying the behavior of rapidly moving electrons emitted in the radioactive decay of the element radium. Among the atoms of a sample of radium are some that disintegrate spontaneously. As they disintegrate, such radioactive atoms emit tiny particles known as electrons. The electron, discovered in 1897 by the British physicist J. J. Thomson, is the least massive charged particle known, and it carries a negative electrical charge. Because of its small mass it is relatively easy to accelerate an electron in an electrical or magnetic field, and this is what Kaufmann was doing. He was testing a model of the electron that had been proposed by the great Dutch physicist Hendrik Lorentz. In this model, Lorentz visualized the electron as being a tiny, electrically charged sphere. According to Lorentz, when such a sphere was set in motion, it was "flattened" by the same contraction that Lorentz had suggested as being necessary to preserve the concept of the ether in his studies of the speed of light. But Lorentz also reasoned that as the electron was set in motion, its mass would increase. Lorentz had presented all of these concepts in terms of his special model of electromagnetic forces. Lorentz did not realize that what he was doing was simply a very special case of Einstein's theory. Kaufmann wanted to test the mass increase alleged by Lorentz's theory. In his paper, he came to the conclusion that what he called the "Einstein-Lorentz" theory was wrong! It disagreed with experimental findings. When Lorentz heard about these results he was ready to give up his theory. But when Einstein heard about them he was sure that Kaufmann's experiment was wrong.

He felt that his own theory was so harmonious and explained so many things that it simply had to be right. This is a remarkable attitude, and one that Einstein had throughout most of his life.

A wonderful illustration of this attitude comes in a scene described by Ilse Rosenthal-Schneider, one of Einstein's assistants. It took place in 1919 and involved the news that observations to be described in the next chapter confirmed Einstein's theory of gravitation. Rosenthal-Schneider wrote, "When I was giving expression to my joy that the results [of the observations] coincided with his calculations, he said quite unmoved, 'But I knew that the theory is correct'; and when I asked what if there had been no confirmation of his prediction he countered... 'Then I would have been sorry for the dear Lord—the theory is correct." During the years when Einstein was actively working in physics, his instinct about what had to be true was essentially unerring. He did not ignore experiments, but he had an uncanny ability to sense which of them were to be trusted and which were not. In the case of Kaufmann's original experiments, for example, several years passed before scientists generally agreed that they had been wrongly interpreted, and that newer experiments confirmed the theory of relativity.

Einstein was not the only one who had confidence in his theory. The great German theoretical physicist Max Planck, who was at the University of Berlin and who probably saw Einstein's paper in manuscript form, was so taken by it that he asked a student there, Max von Laue, to prepare a colloquium on it for the winter term of 1905–06. Von Laue was in turn so taken by the theory that he made a special trip to Bern to meet Einstein. He was astonished to discover that he and Einstein were the same age. He had expected to encounter a senior scientist. Einstein later remarked that von Laue was actually the first real physicist he had ever met in person. (Incidentally, von Laue was awarded the Nobel Prize in physics in 1914, seven years before Einstein won his Nobel Prize.) Einstein's isolation in Bern was such that he did not even have access to a significant physics library. Soon after the colloquium, Planck began lecturing on the theory of relativity, and he appears to have had the first student ever awarded a Ph.D. for a problem connected with it.

Ultimately, Einstein's most controversial work in physics during the miracle year of 1905 was to create the theory of the quantum, the particle nature of light, by extending work that Planck had begun. As we will see, the quantum theory leads us into much deeper waters than relativity does—so deep, in fact, that Einstein eventually decided not to swim in them himself. But to many of his contemporaries, the most controversial

The German physicist Max Planck is considered the father of the quantum theory. He and Einstein later became colleagues in Berlin.

aspect of Einstein's work in 1905 may, from our current vantage point, seem absurd: That was the question of whether or not atoms "exist." What could one possibly mean by such a question? Ernst Mach, who did not believe that atoms existed, used to ask people who did believe in them, "Have you seen one lately?" Although we now have "pictures" of atoms taken by special high-powered microscopes, these pictures are very remote from our everyday experience without an explanation of what they represent. Most of us believe that atoms exist because the model of the atom that we have seen in books and the popular media explains so much about them. This is where the argument was. Both believers and disbelievers agreed that thinking of matter as being made up of atoms explained a lot of things, but were there really "solid, massy, hard, impenetrable, moveable particles," as Newton had said?

By the end of the 19th century there were actually two models of the atom: one for chemists and one for physicists.

Chemists used a model that explained why the chemical elements combined with one another in particular proportions. If, for example, we think of the water molecule as being composed of two hydrogen atoms and one oxygen atom, the electrical properties of hydrogen atoms and of oxygen atoms enable us to understand why two volumes of hydrogen combine with one volume of oxygen to give us one volume of water. For this purpose the size, shape, and mass of the atoms do not make any difference. The 19th-century physicist's model of the atom, on the other hand, had to include all of these attributes, and it had to include them in detail. For example, a physicist would want to know that a hydrogen atom has a mass of about 10^{-24} grams. It is the measurement of such properties that has since convinced us of the reality of atoms.

In the 19th century, physicists including James Clerk Maxwell and the great Austrian theoretical physicist Ludwig Boltzmann used the existing model of the atom to relate such "thermodynamic" quantities as the temperature and pressure of a gas to the average behavior of the molecules of which they assumed the gas was made. In the case of a fixed volume of gas, for example, the increase in its pressure that accompanies an increase in its temperature was explained by the collisions of the molecules of the gas with the wall of the container holding the gas. An increase in temperature increases the energy and the average speed at which these molecules fly around. The result is an increase both in the number of times per second that the molecules collide with the container walls and the increasing momentum they transfer to the walls in each collision, thereby increasing the pressure on the walls of the container. That is the molecular explanation for the fact that the pressure increases as the temperature increases. One could not possibly follow the motions of each of the 10^{19} or so molecules in every cubic centimeter of a gas. What scientists do is study the average behavior of these molecules, a discipline that became known as "statistical mechanics." Statistical mechanics was one of Einstein's great loves. He kept coming back to it again and again during the course of his career. Indeed, three of the papers he published in the *Annalen* prior to 1905 were on this subject. If his career had stopped right there he might have merited only a footnote in the history of this subject since, unknown to him, much of his work had already been done by others, especially by the American master Willard Gibbs, at Yale University.

Two of Einstein's papers in the miracle year had to do with statistical mechanics and the existence of atoms. There was no question in Einstein's mind that atoms existed. Though he had a good deal of respect for Mach as a philosopher, one gets the impression that Einstein felt that Mach's objections to the atomic theory were a little silly. The two papers Einstein published on statistical mechanics in 1905 had to do with what is now called "Brownian motion." Robert Brown was a Scottish botanist who, in the summer of 1827, began to study the pollen grains from various plants when these particles were immersed in water. Since a typical pollen grain has a length of a tiny fraction of a millimeter, Brown had to observe their behavior through a microscope. What he noticed was that the pollen grains continually jiggled around in the water. At first Brown thought that the grains might actually be alive. But when he repeated the experiment with dried pollen grains that had been preserved for about 20 years, he found that they also jiggled. So did microscopic particles of gum resin, coal tar, manganese, nickel, bismuth, and arsenic, among other substances. In fact *anything* appeared to jiggle when suspended in the form of tiny grains in a liquid. This apparently random movement is now called "Brownian motion."

To at least some of the 19th-century atomists, the correct explanation for Brownian motion seemed apparent—it was caused by collisions, countless collisions per second, of invisible water molecules with the visible, microscopic particles of a substance. But it was Einstein who first made this subject into a quantitative science.

What does it take to make this subject quantitative? If you follow the motion of a single grain of a substance, you will see that it performs what has come to be called a "random walk." If you were such a grain and were continuously being bombarded by smaller molecules coming from all sides at random, how would you move? The first collision would carry you a step in one direction, and the next collision would carry you a step in another direction. It is totally improbable that the second collision would take you back to the point from which you originally began. And then a third collision would carry you a step in yet another direction still farther from where you began. Einstein's theory predicts the average distance (but not the direction) that you would move from where you began within a given time. The result is a little surprising. The distance, rather than increasing directly with time, increases in proportion to the square root of the time. For example, to go twice as far you have to wait four times as long. This formula reflects the random nature of your movement, with some collisions carrying you generally forward and others generally backward.

This prediction cries out to be tested. Indeed, it was tested in a series of experiments begun in 1908 by the French physicist Jean Perrin, for which he received the Nobel Prize in 1926. Perrin's work convinced almost all physicists that atoms really do exist. But they did not convince Mach. Soon after his death in 1916, his son Ludwig found the following passage among his father's papers: "I do not consider the Newtonian principles as completed and perfect; yet in my old age I can accept the theory of relativity just as little as I can accept the existence of atoms and other such dogma."

The work for which Einstein finally did win the Nobel Prize is found in his first paper of the miracle year, published in March 1905. It was somewhat dauntingly entitled

"Concerning a Heuristic Point of View about the Creation and Transformation of Light." The dictionary definition of "heuristic" is "providing aid and direction in the solution of a problem but otherwise unjustified or incapable of justification." Why would Einstein describe his viewpoint as "heuristic," or incapable of justification? He certainly did not think that the theory of relativity was incapable of justification. Quite to the contrary, he believed it so capable of justification that he was prepared to ignore experiments that seemed to disagree with it. Furthermore, why did Einstein, writing to his Olympia Academy comrade Conrad Habicht in a 1905 letter about his work, focus on this paper, among all those he published in that miracle year, as being "very revolutionary"? One reason was that to Einstein, the theory of relativity was not revolutionary at all, but simply a careful reformulation of classical physics, but taking into account that light does not travel instantaneously from one place to another. Einstein would very probably have had no trouble in explaining relativity to Maxwell, even though Maxwell was an ether person. Lorentz, who certainly was an ether person, did eventually accept and embrace relativity. But almost none of these classical physicists—including Einstein himself—could fully accept the implications of these new ideas about light. Why?

As we have seen, most of the optical experiments devised in the 19th century could be readily explained by treating light as a continuous wave. But in the 1860s, experimental physicists began to examine what became known as "cavity" or "blackbody" radiation (see sidebar).

By the end of the last century measurements of the blackbody spectrum became available, and here the trouble began. Theorists started to look for a formula that could describe the color distribution of the blackbody spectrum emerging from a cavity, and finally Max Planck found an equation that seemed to fit perfectly. The problem was how to justify it, or derive it from physical principles. Planck

text continues on page 82

I n the 1860s a German physicist named Gustav Kirchhoff, who was at the University of Heidelberg and who eventually became Planck's teacher in Berlin, carried out a series of experiments on the emission and absorption of light. Out of his physical description of this process grew the concept of "cavity" or "blackbody" radiation.

The idea is very simple. Take a cylindrical tube of some sort of metal. One end is closed, and the other has a small hole to let light in or out. If the tube is at room temperature, any light that goes in the hole will tend to get trapped inside. If you look at the hole, it will appear black. Hence the radiation trapped inside is usually called blackbody radiation. On the other hand, if you heat the tube, the surface will glow. But the radiation coming out of the hole will glow even brighter. As the temperature increases, its color will change from dark red to bright yellow to intense white.

What is most remarkable is that this distribution of colors, which is associated with a distribution of wavelengths, does not in any way depend on the material the tube is made of. You get the same distribution if you use tungsten or vanadium to make the cavity as long as the temperature remains the same.

It is of special interest to fix the temperature and examine with a spectrometer the intensity of the different wavelengths of light coming out of the hole. You will find that light of all wavelengths is represented, but different wavelengths emerge with different intensities. When we say that the hole glows orange, for example, we do not mean that only light with wavelengths corresponding to orange emerges. What we mean is that the most intense light has wavelengths corresponding to orange.

We can make a plot at a given temperature of the intensities that correspond to the different wavelengths (see figure 11). This gives us a curve—a spectrum—that rises to a maximum at some color like orange and then falls off rapidly to zero as the wavelengths get shorter (or equivalently, as the frequency of the light gets larger). This plot is called a blackbody spectrum. Physicists who look at the curve can tell from its shape what the temperature of the blackbody is.

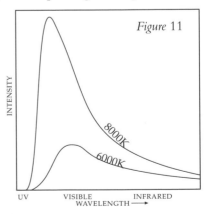

Figure 11

By the end of the 19th century, measurements of the blackbody spectrum were available. Another physicist from the University of Berlin, Wilhelm Wien, produced a formula (on what turned out to be very shaky grounds) that seemed to fit the data. It was at this point that Max Planck enters our story. Planck became obsessed by the blackbody spectrum. It seemed to have the universal property that he liked. It was the same for all substances.

Planck's first idea was to find a better derivation for Wien's formula. He thought he had one, and in 1899 he submitted a paper to the *Annalen der Physik*. But while he was correcting the proofs, he realized that the derivation was wrong. Furthermore, it became increasingly apparent that Wien's formula did not fit the experimental results for the longer wavelengths. Planck then produced a second formula—what has become known as the Planck blackbody distribution. This one fit perfectly, and is the one we have used ever since.

But how to derive it? Here we need a better picture of how radiation behaves inside the cavity. The electrons in the metal making up the walls oscillate back and forth when they are heated. When a charged particle like an electron oscillates, it radiates. Hence these oscillating electrons emit electromagnetic radiation. This radiation can in turn be absorbed by the oscillating electrons, then reradiated, and so on, a process that goes on and on except for the occasional loss of a small amount of radiation through the hole, where it can be observed and measured.

Classical mechanics, indeed common sense as well, suggests that these radiation oscillators could take up radiation in any size dose. But to derive his formula, Planck found that he had to assume that the oscillators could only have multiples of some fundamental unit of energy, the quantum.

Planck's oscillators vibrate with some basic frequency we can call ν. To make this into an energy, Planck had to introduce a constant—we now call it Planck's constant h. It was a new fundamental constant that became one of the defining constants of the universe, such as the speed of light or the charge on the electron. In terms of Planck's constant, the basic energy unit or quantum is $h\nu$. That is, Planck's oscillators could absorb or emit energy only in whole units of $h\nu$. Although Planck remained very uncomfortable with this seemingly arbitrary requirement, it has become the foundation for the 20th-century science of quantum mechanics.

text continued from page 79

found a way, but it seemed entirely self-contradictory. To predict the energy at different wavelengths (and wavelengths imply the use of the *continuous* wave nature of light), he had to assume that light was emitted or absorbed in discrete packets or quanta.

To see why this poses a problem, let's use a homey example. Suppose we replace the radiation by beer, and consider the buying and selling of beer. There is no reason to suppose that some law of nature is working to stop us from buying and selling beer in any quantity we like. We might use pints and quarts, but that would be a matter of convenience. Nothing could stop us from using an eighth of a quart, or even one over the square root of two quarts as our basic unit, if we felt like it. This freedom is exactly what Planck had to abandon to derive his formula. He had to suppose that beer (radiation!) could be "bought" or "sold" only in multiples of some fundamental unit of energy—a quantum of energy as it came to be called. Planck had no justification for this, except that it worked. It led to the correct formula. It was "heuristic."

Planck didn't like this at all. He spent the next ten years trying to find a derivation of his formula that did not use the quantum, but he failed completely.

This was the situation that confronted Einstein in 1905. It is not clear how familiar Einstein was with this earlier work, but he seemed to know a good deal about it. In his paper on the nature of light he does not try to derive Planck's law. He simply accepted it as true and asked what it meant. The conclusion was revolutionary. It means, Einstein decided, that the radiation in a blackbody cavity consists of quanta of energy. As he puts it in his paper, "phenomena related to the generation and transformation of light can be understood better on the assumption that the energy in light is distributed discontinuously in space." According to this concept, "the energy in a beam of light emanating from a point source is not distributed continuously over larger and larger volumes of space but consists of a finite number of energy quanta, localized at points of space, which move without subdividing and which are absorbed and emitted only as units." In other words, not only is beer consumed in pints and quarts, but even within a beer barrel it is neatly packaged in pints and quarts, with nothing in between!

But isn't light a wave? What is this business about light moving around in quanta? Is this some particle theory of light? The situation is even worse than that. According to Einstein, the energy contained in a quantum packet of light, E, is related to the frequency of the light by the formula $E = h\nu$. Here ν is the frequency of the light and h is a new constant that had already been introduced by Planck. But Einstein is saying that any light beam with light of frequency ν is made up of a collection of quanta, each with an energy of $h\nu$. But frequency has to do with the concept of a wave. We measure the frequency of a light wave by counting how many times a second a wave crest passes by us. In Einstein's equation, we seem to be using the wave nature of light to define the energy of the quantum.

Einstein was fully aware of the dilemma of whether light consisted of waves or streams of quanta. It is probably correct to say that in 1905 he was the only person on earth who was fully aware of it. For the rest of his life he thought endlessly about it, and in one of his last letters to Michele Besso, in 1951, Einstein wrote, "All these fifty years of pondering have not brought me any closer to answering the question, What are light quanta?" Later in the book, we will return to this question. But in 1905, fortunately, Einstein did not let it stop him. He took the Planck distribution as a given and asked what it implied. The dual nature of light is evident in Planck's formula if, following Einstein, one knows how to look at it.

Einstein focused on the short-wavelength or high-energy end of the spectrum, and here he was able to use his beloved statistical mechanics. He showed that the light quanta at the high-energy end of the spectrum behave as if they were particles in a gas, following the same principles of behavior as set forth by statistical mechanics. Although there are subtle differences between a gas made up of light quanta and a gas made up of electrons, both behave like gases made up of independent particles. Einstein then went on to suggest how this idea could be tested. In particular, he showed that if light quanta collided with a metal surface, electrons would be ejected from it with an energy that depended on the wavelength—the color—of the light. The "bluer" the light, the more energetic are the ejected electrons. This is known as the "photoelectric effect" and it has all kinds of applications—including the automatic opening of doors. It was for this work that Einstein won the Nobel Prize 16 years later.

LIGHT QUANTA

ach quantum of light contains an energy E = hν, where E is the
energy, h is Planck's constant, and ν the frequency. In relativity
there is a connection between energy and momentum. As applied
to this situation, the connection says that each light quantum has a
momentum, p, expressed by the equation p = hν/c. Since the wave
length and frequency of light are connected by the relation νλ = c, we
can also write this as p = h/λ. This meant to Einstein that if light quanta collided with something, they could transfer their energy and
momenta in a manner similar to that of billiard balls. (Not exactly like
billiard balls, however, since the quanta move with the speed of light.)

If we go back to Einstein's formula that gives the mass of an object
as a function of its speed

$$m = \frac{m_o}{\sqrt{1-v^2/c^2}}$$

we see that the only way in which this formula can be universally true
for a quantum of light—which moves at the speed of light—is if the
quantum has no rest mass! In other words, light quanta are massless particles that nonetheless carry energy and momentum, something a classical physicist would have found incomprehensible. If, for example, such
a quantum hits an electron, it can cause the electron to recoil even
though the quantum has no mass. This was first observed for free electrons by the American physicist Arthur Compton in 1922. It was
Compton who first established that the light quanta carry momenta
given by hν/c. In his 1905 paper, Einstein focused on electrons that
were bound in metal surfaces.

The effect of light on such surfaces had been noticed as early as
1887 by the German physicist Heinrich Hertz. Hertz was studying the
discharge of sparks between two metal surfaces held close together. In
such a case there will generally be a potential difference—a difference in

continues on page 86

continued from page 85

voltage drop—between these two electrical conductors, and if this difference is large enough, an electrical
current will flow between them,
taking the form of a spark.
What Hertz noticed was that
the light from such a spark
itself appeared to generate a
second spark, as if the light
impinging on the metal
released an electrical current.
This is now called the "photo-
electric effect." Hertz noticed
that ultraviolet light was especially
effective in producing this sec-
ondary discharge, but he did not have
an explanation for it and it remained a
puzzle.

*German physicist Heinrich Hertz. He
discovered the photo-electric effect which
Einstein later explained.*

In 1902 the German physicist Philipp
Lenard studied the same effect by shining
light produced by a carbon arc on a metal
surface. (Ironically, Lenard, who later became an enthusiastic Nazi and a
mortal enemy of Einstein, won the Nobel Prize for his work on electrons in
Einstein's miracle year of 1905.) Lenard was able to vary the intensity of his
light source. When he did so he observed that no matter how weak the
intensity of the light striking the metal surface, the electrons that it knocked
off the surface emerged with the same energy. This was an unexpected
effect; classical physics suggested that more intense light would produce
more energetic electrons. In reality, more intense light produces more electrons but not more energetic ones. It appeared that what influenced the

energy of the departing electrons was the frequency of the light striking the metal surface. Ultraviolet light produced more energetic electrons than red light.

Einstein was able to explain all of this in one fell swoop with his light quanta. Each quantum carries an energy $h\nu$. If, as must be the case, energy is conserved in the process by which light quanta release an electron from a metal surface, then we have the simple equation $h\nu = E - W$. This means that the energy that the light can supply is all the energy that is available to the electron. Here $h\nu$ is the energy of the light quantum, E is the energy of the electron being liberated, and W is called the "work function," or energy, that is needed to pry the electron from the metal. It was this equation that earned Einstein the Nobel Prize 16 years later. In Einstein's formula, the dependence of the energy of the electron on the frequency of the impinging light is clear. What is also clear is that more intense light means more light quanta and not more energetic light quanta, thus explaining Lenard's observation. The real test of the equation was not made until 1916, when the American physicist Robert Millikan conducted a series of very precise experiments with various metals. It is of particular interest that these experiments also measured Planck's constant. The constant turned out to have the same value that Planck found it to have in blackbody radiation.

CHAPTER 4

Professor Einstein's Happiest Thought

One of the subjects that Einstein worked on during the miracle year had do with the following problem in chemistry. Suppose you dissolve a small amount of sugar in a solution of water. The sugar molecules will then diffuse through the water until they come into a state of equilibrium, or balance, with the water. The sugar and water will be uniformly mixed. The diffusion of the sugar molecules in the water will produce a pressure that can be measured by putting a thin sheet into the solution and letting the sugar molecules hit it as they diffuse.

Einstein produced a theory about this process that enabled him to determine both the size and the number of the sugar molecules in the solution. The number of molecules in what is known as the "mole" of a substance—an amount equal to the molecular weight of the substance in grams—is called Avogadro's number. This number is named for Amedeo Avogadro, an Italian scientist who first conjectured in 1811 that a given volume of any gas at a fixed temperature and pressure would contain the same number of molecules as the same volume of any other gas under the same conditions. Avogadro's number, usually simply called

In 1912, after holding teaching positions in Bern, Zurich, and Prague, Einstein accepted a teaching position at his alma mater, the ETH in Zurich.

N, is now known to high accuracy. It is 6.0220×10^{23}—meaning that there are a lot of molecules in a mole of any substance. Einstein's original calculation of this number, which he published in 1906, contained a mistake, and so he got only 2.1×10^{23}. When he corrected this mistake a few years later, the number turned out to be closer to the number obtained from experiment.

Einstein submitted his 1905 calculation to the dean of the University of Zurich in July of that year as his Ph.D. thesis. By this time he had already written the papers on relativity and the quantum that created much of 20th-century physics. The notion of his getting a doctorate, implying that he was still a student, seems almost absurd. But then, as now, serious researchers in the sciences were expected to get this advanced degree. As was and still is customary, Einstein's thesis was read by a senior professor at the university, in this case a man named Alfred Kleiner. Kleiner did not notice Einstein's mistake in calculating Avogadro's number, and the thesis was accepted.

Kleiner must have become aware fairly soon that Einstein was not the typical physics student. Almost at once he set about trying to bring Einstein to the University of Zurich. In the meantime, Einstein was promoted in 1906 to the rank of technical expert second class at the patent office, with an annual salary of 4,500 Swiss francs. In his "spare time" he also wrote a paper that created the modern quantum theory of solids. In this paper Einstein took up the problem of how a solid absorbs heat. His innovation was to imagine the electrons in the solid as an array of quantum mechanical oscillators, "springs" that take up and give off energy in quantum units, which in this case absorbed heat energy rather than radiation. This produced a theory that was in substantial agreement with experiments, and convinced many physicists that the quantum theory demanded attention.

Kleiner's strategy for bringing Einstein to Zurich was a

bit indirect. At that time, European universities had a peculiar junior position called a *Privatdozent*—a kind of private teacher. An individual chosen to be a *Privatdozent* was given the right to give lectures at a university, and was paid only a small fee by the students who attended them. The university paid nothing. The money was so little that no one could live on it, but to get a real academic job one had, as a rule, to go this route. Kleiner wanted Einstein to become a *Privatdozent* at the University of Bern, reasoning that if things then went well, he could bring him to Zurich. In the beginning things did not go well. In fact they did not go at all.

For some reason Einstein failed to meet one of the requirements for the job. A candidate was supposed to submit a piece of original research that had not yet been published. The reason for this seemingly unnecessary requirement is not clear. It was apparently not clear to Einstein either, since he did not meet it for two years. In the meantime, apart from his job at the patent office, he expressed some interest in getting a job teaching in a high school. But finally, in 1908, he did submit the required document and was appointed a *Privatdozent* at the University of Bern, while keeping his job at the patent office, which was what really supported himself and his family.

One gets the impression that Einstein was not an especially good classroom teacher, at least on a level that was suitable for the average student. During this period he was too full of original ideas to prepare lectures on standard subjects. Indeed, he must have realized that much of what was being taught in these courses was simply wrong—having been made obsolete by his own work. At one point Kleiner visited Einstein's class at Bern and told him that he thought the lectures were somewhat too advanced. Einstein more or less told Kleiner to mind his own business, remarking that he was not asking to be appointed a professor in Zurich anyway. Kleiner had the good sense to persist, and in 1909

Einstein was made an associate professor at the University of Zurich with a salary of 4,500 Swiss francs a year—the same salary he had been making at the patent office, from which he then resigned. From 1909 to the end of his career, Einstein was always a professor at one institution or another, but he looked back on his years in the patent office as the happiest and freest of his life. Indeed it was in 1907, while working in the patent office, that Einstein had what he called "the happiest thought of my life."

I will first tell you what this thought was. I think you will be surprised by its apparent simplicity and irrelevance to anything, and then by its profundity. In fact it does not seem at first especially happy at all since, as Einstein later recalled, it involved the image of someone falling off the roof of a house. Suppose you are painting the roof of a house and you slip and fall, taking your paints and paintbrushes with you. Ignoring the fact that you will soon hit the ground, which will disrupt the experiment, and neglecting the resistance of the air, you will see all of the objects that fell off the roof with you staying even with you. This is because anything that falls under the influence of gravity from a point just above the surface of the Earth will—neglecting air resistance—fall with the same acceleration as anything else. This acceleration turns out to be about 9.8 meters per second per second. The expression here contains two "per seconds" because an acceleration is the rate of change of a speed that is itself a rate of change of a distance. It seems as if Galileo was the first person to emphasize this. He claimed to have done experiments in which he dropped objects from the Leaning Tower of Pisa to prove it. It is more likely that this was one of Galileo's thought experiments.

According to Newton's theory of gravitation, this uniform acceleration can be understood in the following way. At the surface of the Earth, any object of mass m is subject to the force of gravitation produced by the Earth, which has a mass M and radius R, as given by Newton's famous formula

$$F = \frac{mMG}{R^2}$$

Here G is Newton's constant of universal gravitation, which, in its peculiar units, is G = 6.6720 x 10^{-11} meters per second per second squared per kilogram. But also according to Newton, F = ma, where a is the acceleration produced by the force acting on an object of mass m. Hence Newton would say

$$F = ma = \frac{mMG}{R^2}$$

If we now cancel the m on either side of the equation, we have

$$a = \frac{MG}{R^2}$$

If you put into this equation the radius of the Earth, which is 6.37 x 10^6 meters, and the mass of the Earth, which is 5.98 x 10^{24} kilograms, you will get the 9.8 meters per second per second given earlier as the rate of acceleration of objects falling from near the Earth's surface.

There are two points to be made here. The first is that what I have just done is not quite correct. I have used the radius of the Earth in the formula. Actually, the hapless painter's distance from the surface of the Earth keeps changing during his fall. But this change is tiny compared to the radius of the Earth, and so I have neglected it. The second point is the really important one and was Einstein's "happiest thought." Without thinking much about it, we have canceled the mass *m* from both sides of the mMG/R^2 = ma equation. But Einstein noted that these two uses of *m* have quite different meanings. The *m* on the right side of the equation, the *ma* side, is a measure of how difficult it is to accelerate an object with a given force. It is a measure of the "inertia" of the object. Hence Einstein called this the "inertial mass." But the mass *m* on the other, or force side of the equation, in the combination *mMG,* is a measure of the strength of gravity. Hence Einstein called this "the gravitational mass." The fact that—neglecting air resistance—objects fall with the same acceleration at the surface of the Earth reflects the fact that the inertial and gravitational masses are the same and therefore cancel out in the equation. Einstein called this phenomenon the "principle of equivalence," the equivalence of inertial and gravitational masses. Einstein probably did not know that a Hungarian physicist—Baron Roland Eötvös—had at about this time already shown experimentally that these two masses were equal to within a difference of approximately one part in 100 million. Today it is known that they are equal to within one part in 100 billion! What did Einstein make of this?

In discussing this, it is important to begin by pointing out that Einstein's 1905 paper on relativity did not deal with either acceleration or gravity. It restricted itself to systems that were moving uniformly with respect to each other. In our train example, if the train starts to accelerate, we know it. If we are not careful we may be knocked to the ground by the acceleration. In this sense accelerated motions appear to be "absolute." The "special" theory of relativity—as Einstein's 1905 version of the theory is known—does not apply to such motions. Moreover, the 1905 paper is really built around electrodynamics, and was in fact called "On the Electrodynamics of Moving Bodies." One of its most important aspects was the unification of electricity and magnetism. Thus, while an electron at rest will attract an oppositely charged object with a purely electrical force, the same electron, if set into uniform motion, will manifest both an electric and magnetic force. An "electro-magnet" of the kind we are all familiar with makes use of the magnetism of moving electrons. If we bring all these electrons to rest, this magnetic effect disappears. The two kinds of forces are aspects of what we call electromagnetism. That moving charges generate magnetic fields was well known prior to Einstein. But his 1905 relativity paper made these relationships clear.

Gravity does not fit into this scheme. It does not seem in any obvious way to be related to a state of motion. But the principle of equivalence does reveal such a connection. It tells us that objects that are falling with an acceleration of 9.8 meters per second per second near the surface of the Earth do not feel the force of gravity. We could imagine attaching a scale to the feet of the painter. Before he falls off the roof the scale might read 175 pounds. But once the painter and scale begin to fall the scale will read zero! The painter is weightless. This struck Einstein, who many years later recalled, "I was sitting in a chair in the patent office in Bern when all of a sudden a thought occurred to me: 'If a person falls freely he will not feel his own weight.' I was startled. This simple thought made a deep impression on me. It impelled me toward a theory of gravitation."

We can begin to grasp the implications of Einstein's realization—and the principle of equivalence—if we consider what has come to be known as the "Einstein elevator." This is an imaginary elevator—an enclosed box in space. We can imagine attaching the elevator to a cable, as in Figure 12 below.

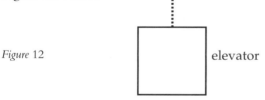

Figure 12   elevator

If we now pull on the cable so that the elevator is accelerated upward with an acceleration of 9.8 meters per second per second, the floor of the elevator will accelerate upward toward any object that was in the elevator. A person inside the elevator will have the sensation of falling down toward the floor with an acceleration of 9.8 meters per second per second, since that is the upward acceleration of the elevator floor.

But we can also give a completely equivalent description of this situation in which the "elevator" sits on the surface of the Earth. Nothing is pulling it up, but gravity is pulling everything down. Objects fall to the floor of the elevator with an acceleration of 9.8 meters per second per second. There is no way of distinguishing this situation from the earlier one. We have two equivalent ways of describing the same phenomenon. Thus, the principle of equivalence is also a kind of relativity principle, but one that involves acceleration and gravity.

A lesser physicist than Einstein might have come this far, but only an Einstein would have taken the next step. Einstein realized that the principle of equivalence implies that gravity alters the fabric of space and time. Let us begin with time. Those of us who live in cities where vehicles move with sirens blaring have all observed the increase in the pitch of the siren when one of these blaring vehicles comes toward us. We also hear the decrease in the siren's pitch when the vehicle moves away from us. This is the Doppler shift for sound waves.

Light waves can also be Doppler-shifted. A most dramatic illustration of this occurs with the expansion of the universe itself. The wavelength of the light coming toward us from distant galaxies is shifted to the red. The wavelength appears longer. We take this to mean that the galaxies are moving away from us. No blue-shifted galaxies have been observed. If the galaxies were all blue-shifted, this would mean that the universe was collapsing! It can be shown (you may have seen a demonstration in your physics class) that for small velocities compared to c the percentage shift in the wavelength of light emitted by a moving object as opposed to the same object when it is not moving is given by v/c, where c is the speed of light. In the case of the Doppler shift for light,

$$\frac{\lambda' - \lambda}{\lambda} = \frac{v}{c}$$

where λ' is the wavelength of light emitted by the moving object and λ is the wavelength of light emitted by the object when at rest. This is the basic formula used to connect the red-shift of galaxies to the speed at which they are receding from us.

Getting back to Earth, let us imagine that in our Einstein elevator we have an atom suspended above the floor that emits light quanta in the direction of the floor. Each light quantum has a wavelength λ. If the elevator is in empty space and is not accelerating, this is the wavelength that we would observe with an apparatus set up on the elevator floor to measure the wavelengths of the incoming light quanta. Now suppose that when the light quanta are emitted, the elevator is accelerated upward with an acceleration of 9.8 meters per second per second. Since the elevator floor is now acquiring a velocity with respect to the light source, the light quanta will appear blue-shifted because of the Doppler effect. The source of the light is moving toward us. But the principle of equivalence tells us that we can replace this arrangement with a stationary elevator sitting at the surface of the Earth, in the Earth's gravitational field. With this arrangement, we will measure a blue shift of exactly the same amount as we would have observed in the accelerated elevator. In other words, gravity changes the color of light! But a light wave is a kind of clock, in that its frequency acts like a clock. This means that gravity alters time! Clocks in a gravitational field run differently from identical clocks in a gravity-free environment.

Einstein thought that one might be able to test this remarkable idea by studying the light emitted by massive stars. As light moves out of the star's gravitational field it should be red-shifted. But because it contains other effects that can change the frequency of starlight, this environment is so complicated that it is very difficult to isolate this effect in stars. The best evidence for Einstein's idea that gravity alters the fabric of time comes from very dense white dwarf stars, and is in general agreement with Einstein's prediction.

However, in the early 1960s, the physicist R. V. Pound

and his collaborators at Harvard performed some experiments that demonstrated Einstein's gravitational light shift
directly. The Jefferson Laboratory at Harvard had a 74-foot
tower. Light could be sent down the tower and observed at
the bottom. Pound's experiment took advantage of the bottom of the tower being 74 feet closer to the center of the
Earth than the top, so that the gravitational attraction is very
slightly stronger at the bottom of the tower than at the top.
The light quanta that were used in the experiment were
generated by a form of iron that is radioactive. The theory
predicted a blue shift of this light of about two parts in
10^{15}—a minuscule shift. But the experimenters were able to
measure it and thus directly confirm Einstein's idea.

To see how gravity alters the geometry of space, we can
again make use of Einstein's elevator. In this case we imagine
that light is allowed to enter one side of the elevator and depart
from the other. Figure 13, below, illustrates this situation.

Figure 13

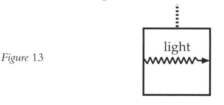

light

Once again we can imagine that the elevator begins to
accelerate upward. Thus, by the time the light leaves the
elevator it will be closer to the floor than it was when it
entered. Figure 14 illustrates the new situation.

Figure 14

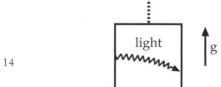

light

g

In effect, the light ray passing through the elevator
appears to have curved toward the floor. Again according to
the principle of equivalence, we can replace this scenario by
an elevator sitting in the gravitational field at the surface of
the Earth. We don't even have to redraw the figure. The

light will be curved just as before. Gravity bends light. We might express the result of what we have just learned by saying that in the presence of gravity, the straight-line path that minimizes the time it takes light to travel from one point to another is "curved." But we would only know this if we could somehow switch off gravity. In order to detect this effect, we could construct a triangle out of three light rays—at least in our imaginations. We could then measure the angles that these light rays make with each other—the interior angles of our triangle. In the absence of gravity we would find that the sum of these angles was 180 degrees, a famous result in Euclidean geometry. But if we were to restore gravity, we would no longer find that this sum was 180 degrees. Space would have become "non-Euclidean." The sum of the angles in our triangle might be greater than 180 degrees or less than 180 degrees, depending on the non-Euclidean geometry that we are dealing with. Since the nature of space is determined by its geometry, we can say, with Einstein, that gravity has "curved" space.

Einstein published a bit about the principle of equivalence in 1907, but did not present the possibility of experimental tests for it until he published a beautiful short paper entitled "On the Influence of Gravitation on the Propagation of Light" in 1911. By this time his personal life had undergone several changes. As we have seen, in 1909 he moved to Zurich to become an associate professor at the university. The following year his second son, Eduard, who was known as "Tede" or "Tedel," was born. This unfortunate child seems to have had psychological problems from the beginning. A sense of the anguish this caused Einstein is conveyed by a letter he wrote to Michele Besso in 1917, when Tede was six: "The state of my youngest son causes me a great deal of concern. It is out of the question that some day he can become a man like others. Who knows, perhaps it would be better for him to leave this world before having known life." Can you imagine what it means

text continues on page 102

What characterizes a Euclidean geometry? For most of you this may seem like a silly question since the only geometry you probably have learned about is that of Euclid. But patience! Remember that you were taught that the interior angles of any triangle add up to exactly one hundred and eighty degrees. Let me remind you of the proof. Below is the relevant figure.

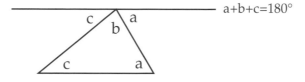

$a+b+c=180°$

Figure 15

Note that in this drawing of a triangle there is a line parallel to the base. In Euclidean geometry there is one, and only one, such line, and the interior angles of the triangle are related in the way that we have seen. A rapid study of the diagram shows why the interior angles of such a triangle add up to 180 degrees. But how do we know that there is such a unique parallel line or, indeed, any parallel line?

In the geometry formulated by Euclid, this is taken as a postulate—an axiom—that is assumed and not proved. But it seemed to many mathematicians who came after Euclid that this so-called fifth postulate was something that ought to be provable from Euclid's other axioms. A sort of cottage industry of incorrect proofs of this proposition flourished for centuries. Early in the 19th century the great German mathematician Carl Friedrich Gauss decided to try a different tack. He attempted, successfully, to construct a geometry that abandoned Euclid's postulate of parallels. In Gauss's geometry, an infinite number of lines run parallel to a given line. Moreover, the sum of the angles of a triangle is less than 180 degrees. Gauss even had the idea of testing to see whether giant triangles formed by light rays joining three stars

The geometry formulated by the Greek mathematician Euclid in the fourth century B.C. went unchallenged until the 19th century, when several new kinds of geometry were constructed.

in space might be non-Euclidean, although it was not clear how this was supposed to have been done in practice. Gauss appears to have been somewhat embarrassed by his non-Euclidean geometry. Indeed, he probably would not have published it in his lifetime except that it was discovered independently by the mathematicians Janos Bolyai and Nikolai Lobachevsky, and that inspired Gauss to claim priority.

In the middle of the 19th century the German mathematician Bernhard Riemann exhibited a geometry in which there were no parallel lines. A model of such a geometry is given by the great circles on the surface of a sphere, while the gaussian geometry can be realized by the lines on a saddle-shaped surface. Riemann unified all of these geometries under a single conceptual umbrella—as Einstein was to rediscover and use a decade after having had his happiest idea.

text continued from page 99

for a father to write in those terms about a son? Tede spent his life in and out of institutions and finally died in one in Switzerland in 1965.

After spending only a year at the University of Zurich, Einstein was appointed a full professor at what was called the German University in Prague—the institution at which Ernst Mach had spent much of his career. This was a very significant appointment that had to be approved by the Austro-Hungarian emperor, Franz Joseph. For the swearing-in ceremony, a new professor needed a special uniform that looked like the uniform of an admiral. When Philipp Frank succeeded Einstein in Prague, Einstein gave the uniform to Frank for his own swearing-in ceremony. It must have been a poor fit, since Einstein was a rather large man and Professor Frank a rather small one.

Professor Frank often told the story of one of his visits to Einstein in Prague. Einstein's office overlooked a park with shady trees and a lovely garden. During the day he would see groups of people in various sorts of animated discussions, sometimes speaking to themselves. Einstein discovered that it was an insane asylum and that these were inmates who did not have to be confined. He pointed this out to Professor Frank and remarked, "Those are the madmen who don't spend their time thinking about the quantum theory."

After a year, Einstein received and accepted an offer from the ETH in Zurich, his alma mater. Perhaps one of the reasons for his move was the growing strain in his married life with Mileva. He may have thought a change of scene would help to save the marriage. It is always very difficult for an outsider to know exactly why a marriage comes apart. Professor Frank saw Einstein and Mileva together, and his writings about them give the impression that he did not like Mileva very much, finding her cold and unresponsive. But some people who knew her strongly disagreed. Before he died in 1973, her older son Hans Albert, who later moved to the United States and became a distin-guished professor of hydraulic engineering at the University of California at Berkeley, remembered his mother as a lov-ing person who was in great need of love herself. Living with Einstein, while it certainly must have had its satisfac-tions, cannot have been easy for a woman. Einstein, once he found his path in physics, never belonged to anyone or anything. He had no special patriotic feelings about the countries in which he lived, and the people around him always had the sense that an important part of him was inaccessible. He spent his life thinking about physics, and that was a journey he had to travel alone.

One part of Einstein's 1911 paper on the influence of gravitation on light has to do with the red or blue shifting of light caused by gravity, and the chances of measuring it in stars, as discussed earlier. The other part of the paper has to due with the role of gravity in bending light rays. This paper makes no mention of what this means for the geome-try of space-time. That would come later. The entire paper is based only on the principle of equivalence. The example Einstein gives involves light from a distant star grazing the surface of the sun. Because of the Sun's gravity the path of the starlight becomes bent, as shown in a highly exagger-ated way in Figure 16.

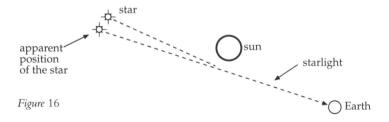

Figure 16

Because of this deflection, the distant star will appear to an observer to have be in a position that is shifted away from the Sun by a tiny angle. Einstein thought of a clever way to measure this. One would photograph a field of stars. Then one would wait for a total eclipse of the Sun by the Moon and photograph those stars in the field whose light passes by the edge of the Sun. Under such circumstances, one would, according to the theory, expect to see a small shift in the apparent positions of the stars in the two cases. Again it was a prediction crying out to be tested. But for reasons to be explained shortly, it was not to be tested for eight years, and then what was tested was not the prediction made in Einstein's 1911 paper, but rather the prediction of his 1916 masterpiece—the theory of general relativity and gravitation—which had superseded it.

Einstein remained at the ETH in Zurich until the spring of 1914. While still lacking the world acclaim he would have five years later, after his general theory of relativity was confirmed, no one who knew anything about it any longer doubted that he was one of the greatest physicists who had ever lived. Consequently, it is not surprising that soon after moving to Zurich he was offered what was probably the most prestigious position in Europe for a theoretical physicist. The University of Berlin had assembled one of the most notable groups of scientists from all disciplines who had ever been housed within a single institution. It included past and future Nobel Prize winners in every field.

Max Planck, the senior professor of theoretical physics, visited Einstein in the spring of 1913 to sound him out about coming to Berlin. The offer was too good to refuse. Einstein would have no teaching responsibilities. By this time he had had enough of teaching. He was engaged in a monumental effort to create a new theory of gravitation, and he wanted to be able to work on it without distractions. Planck also offered Einstein membership in the Prussian Academy of Sciences and the prospect of becoming the director of a planned institute for theoretical physics.

Einstein accepted the offer and moved to Berlin with Mileva and his two sons. They did not stay for long. Within a short time the couple separated for good; Mileva moved back to Switzerland with her sons while Einstein remained in Berlin.

Einstein's first wife, Mileva, with their two sons, Eduard, left, and Hans Albert. Mileva retained custody of the boys after the couple separated in 1914.

They were finally divorced in 1919. One of the conditions of the divorce was that Mileva would receive the proceeds of any Nobel Prize that Einstein might win in the future.

After Mileva left, Einstein moved into a bachelor apartment. He became acquainted—or reacquainted—with some wealthy, conservative Berlin relatives who had previously thought of him as something of an irresponsible absentminded scientist. But he was now a professor at what was arguably the most distinguished scientific institution in the world. The head of the family, Rudolf, was a cousin of Einstein's father. He had a daughter, Elsa, whom Einstein had known since childhood. They were about the same age. She had married a man named Lowenthal with whom she had had two daughters, Ilse and Margot. The Lowenthals had gotten divorced, and Einstein and his cousin Elsa began spending an increasing amount of time together.

Einstein made his formal introductory address to the Prussian Academy in July 1914. In August, World War I broke out. The next few years were both extremely difficult and extremely exciting for Einstein. He hated the war and above all what he considered the mindless patriotism of his German colleagues. When the war broke out they produced a document called "Manifesto to the Civilized World." In it they proclaimed that anyone who accepted German culture would also have to accept the German military ideal, since it was part of the culture. Ninety-three prominent German scientists, artists, musicians, and writers, including Planck, signed it. Einstein refused. On the contrary, he joined antimilitarists in other countries to try, without success, to stop the war.

In 1915 Einstein visited one of these anti-militarists, the French writer Romaine Rolland, who was living in exile in Switzerland. Rolland described the visit in his diary, and his description provides a good sense of how Einstein appeared in his mid-30s, when he was reaching the height of his creative powers. Rolland wrote, "Einstein is still a young man, not very tall, with a wide and long face, and a great mane of crisp, frizzled and very black hair, sprinkled with gray and rising high from a lofty brow. His nose is fleshy and prominent, his mouth small, his lips full, his cheeks plump, his chin rounded. He wears a small cropped mustache. He speaks French rather haltingly, interspersing it with German. He is very much alive and fond of laughter. He cannot help giving an amusing twist to the most serious thoughts."

Rolland continued, "Einstein is incredibly outspoken in his opinion about Germany, where he lives and which is his second fatherland (or his first). [One can understand Rolland's confusion. Einstein was a German citizen by birth. He then became a Swiss citizen by choice. It is possible that by becoming a member of the Prussian Academy in 1913 he automatically became a German citizen as well. In 1940 Einstein became an American citizen, but still retained his Swiss citizenship.] No other German acts and speaks with a similar degree of freedom. Another man might have suffered from a sense of isolation during that terrible last year [while the war was raging], but not he. He laughs. He has found it possible, during the war, to write his most important scientific work."

However carefree Einstein may have appeared to Rolland, the events of the war years took a toll on his health. First, he had the worry of his family in Switzerland. Second, he had the problem of inadequate food in Germany, although as a Swiss citizen he was entitled to, and did, receive food packets from Switzerland. And third, he was engaged in a monumental effort to formulate a new theory of gravitation to replace Newton's. It is little wonder that he developed a stomach ulcer that kept him in bed for substantial periods. Things would have been much worse had it not been for Rudolf and his family—especially Elsa. She came to look after his well-being. Above all she made sure that he ate properly.

In the summer of 1917 Einstein moved from his original apartment to one next to Elsa's, and a year later they decided to get married. It was at this point that he began formal divorce proceedings against Mileva. Apparently she never reconciled herself to the divorce, and it left a residue of bitterness that lasted for the rest of her life. Einstein wrote much later, "This darkened the relations to my two boys, to whom I was attached with tenderness. This tragic aspect of my life continued undiminished until my advanced age." The days of "schatzerl" and "doxerl" had vanished like last year's snow.

None of these personal concerns kept Einstein from thinking about physics. Almost from the time he published his 1911 paper on the principle of equivalence, Einstein realized that it could not represent a final theory of gravitation. The most significant limitation of the principle is that it applies to a very restricted class of gravitational interactions—so restricted that they are never found in nature—at least not exactly in the way stated by the principle. The principle of equivalence contemplates a gravitational force that is constant in space. It is referred to as a "uniform" gravitational field. But no real gravitational field is uniform. Even the gravitational field at the surface of the Earth is not uniform. Apart from the variation in the gravitational force caused by the failure of masses to be uniformly distributed in and on the Earth, the gravitational force also depends on one's height above the surface of the Earth. This was the effect used by R. V. Pound and his associates at Harvard in the experiments we discussed earlier. If we ignore these variations, arguing that such effects occur over very large distances compared to the region within which we are doing our experiments, the principle of equivalence give us approximately correct results for many purposes. But it is not true in general. This Einstein realized in 1911. But what to do about it?

The special theory of relativity deals with transformations of space and time coordinates from an observer at rest to an observer moving uniformly. The principle of equivalence deals with transformations between an observer at rest in a uniform gravitational field and an observer free of gravitation but accelerating uniformly. What Einstein decided was needed was a theory that allowed any transformation of space-time variables for any such situation. At first, he did not have the necessary mathematics to construct such a theory. He appears to have studied some of this mathematics as a student in the ETH, but he had not paid much attention to it and had forgotten it. However, Einstein knew a fellow student at the ETH, Marcel Grossman, who had not forgotten. Grossman played an important role at various moments in Einstein's life. His meticulous notes helped Einstein to pass examinations at the ETH. Grossman's father was the person who recommended Einstein for his job in the patent office. It was Grossman, who had become dean of the mathematics and physics section of the ETH, who persuaded Einstein to return there in 1912. And now it was Grossman to whom Einstein turned for help with the mathematics for his all-encompassing transformation theory.

Grossman was not a specialist in the kind of small-region geometry that Einstein needed. But Grossman soon discovered that Bernhard Riemann, the German mathematician responsible for one type of non-Euclidean geometry, had formulated a general theory of these geometries. Riemann was an extraordinary mathematical genius who died in 1866 of tuberculosis at scarcely the age of 40. When he was in his late 20s he gave a lecture on the foundations of geometry in which he presented the essential ideas of what we now call "Riemann space." The key idea of a Riemann space is that one should be able to define the "distance" between any two of its points. I have put "distance" in quotations because in relativity, both space and time must be included, and the distance it involves is the "distance" between two points, or "events," as they are called in space-time. The Riemann space relevant to relativity is a four-dimensional space with three space dimensions and one time dimension, although— as will shortly be seen—it may not always be possible to distinguish between space and time.

To go into a bit more detail, the distance between two events is defined in terms of what we call a "metric." A very simple example of a metric is the distance between a point that we can label with the coordinates (x,y) and the origin of our coordinate system, which has the coordinates (0,0), as shown in Figure 17.

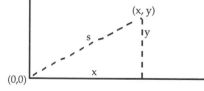

Figure 17

If we call this distance s, then from the Pythagorean theorem we have

$$s^2 = x^2 + y^2$$

What Riemann realized was that if the space in which the coordinates exist is taken to be non-Euclidean, the metric becomes more complicated. Indeed, each metric defines a different non-Euclidean geometry, some appropriate to spheres, some to saddles, some to other surfaces. In his lecture, Riemann even seemed to conjecture that the structure of the actual metric of space—he did not know about relativity and so was talking about space and not space-time— depends on the "forces acting on it." This is exactly what Einstein discovered.

Making the complete connection between gravitation and geometry took Einstein another three years. These were the most intense three years of work that Einstein ever did. Why were they so hard? While Riemann and others had made a pass at the mathematics of non-Euclidean space, Einstein, at first with the help of Grossman and then by himself, had to put it in a useful form. If you look at Einstein's paper entitled "The Foundation of the General Theory of Relativity," which he published in 1916, you will see that most of it is a kind of mathematics lesson. He had to teach the reader the mathematics of Riemann and his successors. This was entirely unfamiliar to most physicists, and it is unlikely that any mathematician had put it together in the detail with which Einstein did. People who have not read this paper sometimes say that Einstein was a poor mathematician. Indeed, Einstein himself used to joke about his mathematics. But when he needed advanced mathematics he was able to invent or borrow it, just as Newton had done in creating his own theory of gravitation.

The second, and perhaps the most important reason for the difficulty of Einstein's three-year project was that it forced him to give up the clear distinction between space and time that is so fundamental to special relativity. In the absence of gravity, space and time are distinct entities. In the metric of special relativity they play distinctive roles. But in the presence of gravity the metric is altered, and space and time become mixed up with one another. The metric has four coordinates, but the space and time coordinates become entangled. Only when gravity is weak can they be distinguished in a useful way. This was a very difficult conceptual hurdle for Einstein. He had to learn to think in terms of the four-dimensional non-Euclidean geometry of space-time.

How can one test such a theory? Its predictions have to do with how things move under the influence of gravity. In Newton's theory we predict how things move by writing down the equation F = ma and then solving it. But in Einstein's theory there is really no force. What happens is that gravity determines the geometry—the metric—of space-time. This metric defines what is meant by a "straight line" connecting two points in space-time. We have seen that such a line is not the straight line of Euclidean geometry. If we make triangles of such lines the triangles will not obey Euclid's axioms. What matters is that the straight lines—called "geodesics"—are well-defined and can be determined in principle from the gravitational field. An object, whether light or something else, moves along one of these gravity-determined straight lines as it travels from one point to another. This is the general idea in Einstein's theory of space-time. The mathematics is another matter.

The first thing Einstein had to do was to verify that if the gravitational field in a space-time metric is weak, one can, to a first approximation, recover Newton's law. For most applications of space-time Newton's law is perfectly adequate. We must make sure that we don't simply throw it overboard. Einstein was able to confirm that his equations reduced to Newton's equations when gravity is weak. The new physics comes in the next approximation. Here, remarkably, Einstein discovered that his theory had in a certain sense already been confirmed. In 1854 the French astronomer Urbain Leverrier discovered that the orbit of the planet Mercury did not seem to obey Newton's law of gravity. Newton's law predicts that under the influence of the Sun's gravitational field, the orbit of a planet like

Mercury should be a closed ellipse. But the elliptical orbits of Mercury did not appear to close. If one could trace its orbits over millennia by letting the planet draw them in space, the orbits would look like the petals of a flower rather than a single ellipse. In dealing with planets and similar bodies, astronomers like to pick a single point on their orbit and see how that point changes annually. The point they usually pick is the point of the orbit closest to the Sun—the so-called perihelion. Leverrier discovered an advance, or shift, in the perihelion, over and above what could be explained by the disturbance of the planet's orbit by its gravitational attraction to the other planets as well as the Sun, of 38 seconds of arc per century. Later observations confirmed this effect but increased it to 43 seconds of arc per century. Leverrier was at a loss to explain this. One explanation he considered was the presence of some undiscovered planet that was disturbing Mercury's orbit. He even had a name for it—Vulcan. It was never found.

Others suggested arbitrary modifications to Newton's law of gravitation to explain Leverrier's observation. But Einstein now had a new theory of gravitation with a precisely specified correction to Newton's law. He used it to calculate the advance of the perihelion of Mercury from first principles. When he did so he reached a result in essentially perfect agreement with Leverrier's astronomical measurements. He later said, "For a few days, I was beside myself with joyous excitement." One can understand why. He now knew that his theory had to be right. It was the first great advance in the understanding of gravitation since Newton.

Einstein could also use his new theory to reexamine the bending of starlight by the Sun's gravitation. When he did the calculation for this, he discovered that it predicted twice the apparent displacement of those stars whose light passes near the Sun during an eclipse as had been predicted by his 1911 principle of equivalence calculation. What was needed to observe this effect was an eclipse. In fact there had been a total eclipse of the sun in the Crimea in Russia in August 1914. Indeed, a colleague of Einstein's, the astronomer Erwin Freundlich, had been inspired by Einstein's 1911 paper to go to the Crimea in 1914 to measure the deflection of starlight by the Sun. But his expedition was caught up in the outbreak of the World War I, and while its members survived intact, they did not get to observe the stars.

Not until 1919 was Einstein's prediction actually tested. In 1917, the British Astronomer Royal, F. W. Dyson, had suggested that the British mount expeditions in 1919, when there would be another eclipse of the Sun. In any event, there were two expeditions. One, led by the astronomer Andrew Crommelin, went to Sobral in Brazil. The other, led by Arthur Eddington, went to Principe, an island off the coast of Spanish Guinea. Eddington, a Quaker who had been a conscientious objector during the war, was one of the greatest astrophysicists of the 20th century. For him, the fact that a British expedition was testing the prediction of a "German" scientist truly meant that the war was over. More

Einstein's predictions were first tested in 1919, by observations made during a solar eclipse. During the next solar eclipse, in 1922, another expedition, seen here unloading their supplies, traveled to Australia to confirm that the Sun's gravity bent starlight as Einstein had predicted.

than that, Eddington was a marvelous writer. His account of the expedition to Principe is so graphic that one tends to forget that there even was another expedition. Here is what he wrote in his book, *Space, Time and Gravitation.*

> On the day of the eclipse the weather was unfavorable.... [We obtained sixteen photographs of which only] one was found showing fairly good images of five stars, which were suitable for a determination. This was measured on the spot a few days after the eclipse in a micrometric measuring-machine. The problem was to determine how the apparent positions of the stars were affected by the sun's gravitational field, compared with the normal positions on a photograph taken when the sun was out of the way. Normal photographs for comparison had been taken with the same telescope in England in January. The eclipse photograph and a comparison photograph were placed film to film in a measuring machine so that corresponding images fell close together, and the small distances were measured in two rectangular directions. From these the relative displacements of the stars could be ascertained....
>
> The results from this plate gave a definite displacement in good accordance with Einstein's theory and disagreeing with the Newtonian prediction. [It is not quite clear to what Eddington refers here. Newton himself did suggest that gravity could bend light, which is not greatly surprising, since Newton thought of light as being made up of particles of some sort. However, Newton did not calculate the displacement.] Although [the number of stars examined] was very meager compared with what had been hoped for, the writer (who it must be admitted was not altogether unbiased) believed it convincing.

Einstein's prediction had been a displacement of 1.74 seconds of arc. Eddington's group found a displacement of 1.61 seconds, with an error of .3 seconds. Given the errors, these two numbers overlap. The second expedition found a displacement of 1.98 seconds, also with a small error. This evidence was sufficiently convincing to prompt a joint meeting of the Royal Society and the Royal Astronomical

Society in London on November 6, 1919. Given that Newton, whose theory was being overthrown, had been a prominent member of the Royal Society, the atmosphere at the meeting must have been electric. Something of its flavor was captured by the philosopher-mathematician Alfred North Whitehead, who was present. He wrote, "The whole atmosphere of tense interest was exactly that of the Greek drama. We were the chorus commenting on the decree of destiny disclosed in the development of a supreme incident. There was dramatic quality in the very staging— the traditional ceremonial, and in the background the picture of Newton to remind us that the greatest of scientific generalizations was now, after more than two centuries, to receive its first modification. Nor was the personal interest wanting; a great adventure in thought had at length come safe to shore."

How did Einstein hear of the expedition's results? Communication between Britain and Germany in those postwar days was still rather indirect, but there was a scientific "grapevine," and rumors reached Einstein of a successful test in late October. They were confirmed when he went to Leiden, Holland, to visit Hendrik Lorentz, who had heard the news from Britain. After the official announcement on November 6, Lorentz sent Einstein, who had returned to Berlin, a cable confirming it. In the fall of 1919 Einstein's mother was found to have stomach cancer. She was hospitalized in a clinic in Switzerland. On the day Einstein heard from Lorentz, he sent her a postcard that began "Joyful news today. H. A. Lorentz has telegraphed me that the English expedition has really proved the deflection of light by the sun." At the time of the announcement in London, on November 6, 1919, Einstein became the most famous scientist in the world, and remained so for the rest of his life. He would never be a private individual again.

Einstein in his Berlin home with his second wife, Elsa, and stepdaughter, Margot, in 1929.

Einstein's Cosmology

At the beginning of 1920, Einstein's mother, who was dying, moved into the Einstein's apartment in Berlin, where she spent her last days living in Einstein's study. She died in March of that year. By this time Einstein had settled into a comfortable upper-middle-class apartment and a comfortable upper-middle-class life with Elsa and her two daughters. He became a much-sought-after university professor who lectured all over Europe. Elsa Einstein appears to have been a very caring wife, but something, at least from Einstein's point of view, must have been askew in their marriage. Otherwise he would not have written to Michele Besso's family that what he admired most about Besso was "that he was able to live so many years with one woman, not only in peace but also in constant unity, something I have lamentably failed at twice...."

Why did Einstein feel that his marriage to Elsa was a failure? Did she feel the same way? We don't know. Certainly when Einstein married Elsa he gave up whatever remained of his informal lifestyle. Photographs taken at this time show a well-dressed, sometimes even elegant-looking man. The perhaps more familiar image of Einstein dressed in baggy pants and a sweater come from photographs taken in the years after Elsa's death in 1936. A 1931 photograph taken in Los Angeles while they were married shows Einstein in a tuxedo and Elsa in an evening dress. Next to them is Charlie Chaplin, also in a tuxedo. The three are attending the premiere of Chaplin's film *City Lights.* Elsa's writings suggest that she realized that Einstein's thoughts were usually somewhere in physics and inaccessible to her. This cannot have been conducive to a very intimate relationship between them, and it may be the reason for Einstein's sense of failure about their marriage.

Moreover, with the 1916 publication of Einstein's paper on general relativity and gravitation, he had reached the high mark of his scientific career. This statement has to be put into perspective. For the next decade Einstein did do

Einstein lectures on relativity in Paris, 1922. Einstein received invitations from around the world to present his theory of relativity.

work that for another physicist might have constituted a brilliant and perhaps even Nobel Prize–winning career. However, Einstein was not any other physicist.

His general theory of relativity is so rich in ideas that many people are still devoting their lives to it. The attempt, so far unsuccessful, to reconcile it with the quantum theory is at the forefront of many modern physicists' work. For reasons that will become clear as we proceed, namely Einstein's distaste for the quantum theory, it is not likely that Einstein would have had much if any interest in this work. For several years after his 1916 paper he kept busy exploring some of the consequences of general relativity. Of special interest was his 1917 paper entitled "Cosmological Considerations on the General Theory of Relativity," which founded modern theoretical cosmology.

Cosmology is the working out of the origin and destiny of the universe as a whole. To someone who believes deeply in one of the traditional religions, the origin and destiny of the universe has to do with a system of religious beliefs. But a scientist can confront at least some of these questions using traditional scientific methods and can obtain quantitative answers. To a scientist, what controls the evolution of the universe as a whole is the force of gravitation. Gravity is the weakest force that we know when it acts on conventional masses, such as those measured in grams or kilograms. But because the Earth has a huge mass, and because the effects of all the masses composing the Earth add up, its gravitational attraction will influence even a particle whose motions are otherwise influenced almost completely by electromagnetism.

If we recall that the force of gravity between two masses m and M in Newtonian physics is measured in terms of the constant GmM, where G is Newton's gravitational constant that measures the strength of the force of gravitation, it is not surprising that the collective gravitation of all the masses in the universe influences the way in which the universe evolves.

The first person to examine some of the consequences of this role of gravitation was Newton. Newton was troubled by the following conundrum: Suppose that we have a universe that has a finite extent in space, and that because of the motions of its matter this matter "clumps up" slightly at some place and some point in time. When this happens, Newton argued, more matter will then be drawn to this little clump because of the attractive nature of gravitation. More matter will continue to be drawn to the clump until the entire universe is clumped up at a single place—which is something that we don't observe. Newton decided that the way to resolve this conundrum was to make the universe *infinite* in space, so that there would be no "place" in which the matter would clump. In a letter to a contemporary, Newton wrote that "if matter was evenly distributed throughout an infinite space it would never convene into one mass; but some of it would convene into one mass and some into another, so as to make an infinite number of great masses scattered at great distances from one another throughout all that infinite space."

When Einstein did his work in cosmology in 1917, he had a very different picture of the universe as a whole than we do now. It was then generally believed among astronomers that the Milky Way galaxy—our galaxy—was all that there was to the universe. Only in the next decade, through the research of the American astronomer Edwin Hubble and others, did we realize that our galaxy was only a tiny fraction of the universe. Other galaxies were scattered through space as far as the telescope could see. Einstein also believed—and this was really a philosophical prejudice—that the finite Milky Way universe was static. This view holds that what we see now, as we observe the universe as a whole, is what people always have seen and what they will always see. This is not to say that individual stars such as the Sun do not evolve, but rather that the *average* distribution of matter in the universe as a whole is static.

Having accepted this view, Einstein was confronted in his own theory with the same problem that had troubled Newton—how to keep the matter in the universe from clumping up and collapsing. Rather than making space infinite, as Newton had done, Einstein modified his theory of general relativity, and it was this modification that was the subject of the 1917 paper. It turns out that one can add a term—Einstein referred to it as the "cosmological member"—to the original equations of the relativity theory without destroying their symmetry. The equations become less beautiful because of this arbitrary term, but they still are allowed by the theory. If one formulates this additional term properly it introduces a tiny repulsive force that counteracts gravity. You will not see this force if you stand on a scale, but it can have the effect of keeping static the universe as a whole—of preventing gravitational collapse. A decade or so after the 1917 paper, Einstein would refer to this mutilation of his original theory as his greatest scientific "blunder." Why?

The first clue that he had made a blunder came not from the stars but from Russia. And it came from a man who was not even a professional physicist—a man named Aleksandr Aleksandrovich Friedmann. Friedmann had been born in 1888 into a talented musical family in St. Petersburg. He studied mathematics at the university there and after graduating took up theoretical meteorology. When the war broke out, Friedmann volunteered for the Russian air force, and by the end of the war he was one of the principal figures in the Russian manufacture of aviation instruments. By 1920, still only in his early 30s, Friedmann was back at the university in St. Petersburg teaching physics and mathematics. Like so many others, Friedmann had been caught up in the relativity "boom" that had erupted worldwide after the results of the 1919 eclipse were announced. Unlike most others, Friedmann, despite not being a professional physicist, had the genius not only to understand Einstein's original papers, but to improve on them.

Not having Einstein's prejudice about static universes, Friedmann found an elegant set of solutions to Einstein's original equations, one that allowed the universe to expand or contract. Whether it expands or contracts depends on the amount of gravitating mass it contains. In the two monumental papers that Friedmann published in 1922 and 1924, he considered all the possibilities for contraction and noncontraction. The equations that he derived are still basically the equations that cosmologists use today. Because these papers were published in a German physics journal, they came to Einstein's attention. His reaction to the first one was very strong. He somehow came to the conclusion that it was simply wrong. He went so far as to publish a one-paragraph note in the same journal pointing to what he had decided was Friedmann's "mistake." This is probably the only paper in physics that Einstein ever published that is literally incorrect. Had Einstein's experimental predictions, based on his limited knowledge, been tested at the time, they would have been shown to be wrong. But his note on Friedmann's paper was instead flawed by a basic mathematical mistake.

Why? Was it that Einstein's philosophical prejudices simply got the better of him, or was it the first intimation that his extraordinary ability to intuitively sense the truth in physics was beginning to desert him? Perhaps it was a bit of both. In any event, after receiving a letter from Friedmann Einstein realized that he had been wrong. He then published a brief retraction in which he said that "Mr. Friedmann's results are both correct and clarifying." But this is really beside the point. It is not that Friedmann's results are simply "clarifying," but rather that they suggest an entirely new view of the cosmos—that it evolves in time, expanding or contracting. Indeed, keeping it from doing so in the theory of general relativity requires drastic measures, such as introducing a force that counteracts gravity, as Einstein's arbitrary added term in the equations for the theory had been intended to do. Einstein's scientific "blunder" was his original belief that Friedmann's solutions could not represent reality. Because of a philosophical prejudice, he had been unable to sense that his own theory was trying to tell him that it was a blunder.

Oddly, a model of an expanding universe to which Einstein did not seem to object existed even before Friedmann. Perhaps this was because he considered it a "toy" without any pretensions to describing the real universe. This model had been invented by the Dutch astronomer Wilhelm de Sitter in 1917. In it, the universe has no gravitating matter. It is not surprising that without gravitating matter to hold it together, in this cosmology the universe is expanding. What is harder to accept is that it can expand faster than the speed of light! At first glance one might say that this idea simply violates the basic principles of relativity. But we must be careful. Relativity tells us that no "thing," whether you, me, or a spaceship—can move faster than light. But here we are talking about space, and as Einstein used to say, "space is not a thing." The whole scale of the universe is blowing up like the surface of a balloon. There is nothing in relativity that says that this expansion cannot proceed faster than the speed of light.

For two reasons, this model of the universe remains interesting to us even today. The first has to do with physics and the second with history. Though most cosmologists would agree that we are not currently in a de Sitter epoch (a period in which the expansion is not dominated by gravitating matter), they do believe that not long after the universe was created in the Big Bang it did go through a brief de Sitter epoch that cosmologists call "inflation." It may well be that the recently discovered "ripples" in the radiation left over from the Big Bang reflect some of the turbulence from this epoch.

De Sitter, in a long appendix to his paper, proposed an experimental test for his model. He wrote that "the frequency of light vibrations [coming from distant stars] diminishes with increasing distance from the origin of [their] coordinates. The lines in the spectra of very distant stars or nebulae must therefore be systematically displaced toward the red, giving rise to a spurious positive radial velocity."

In essence, what de Sitter was saying is that if the universe is expanding away from us, the light coming from distant stars will be Doppler-shifted towards the red end of the spectrum. Furthermore, he says that in his model the red shift will increase as the distance of a star or galaxy increases. The farther away the star or galaxy the greater the red shift. We interpret this red shift as a velocity-dependent

Edwin Hubble observes the sky with the 48-inch telescope at the Mt. Wilson Observatory in California. It was Hubble's discovery that the universe is expanding that led Einstein to drop the modification he had proposed to his theory of gravitation.

Doppler effect. It is odd that Friedmann did not call attention to this in his expanding universe models. All of them have the same red shift law and they are much more plausible than de Sitter's model universe. But the point was not lost. In 1929, Edwin Hubble published a seven-page paper entitled "A Relation Between Distance and Radial Velocity Among Extra-Galactic Nebulae." This paper forever changed the way in which we look at the universe. Notice the reference to "Extra-Galactic Nebulae." By 1929 there was no doubt—certainly Hubble had no doubt—that most of the universe lay beyond the Milky Way. By this time, thanks as much to Hubble as to anyone, the distance to several of these extragalactic nebulae had been measured. Hubble could check de Sitter's prediction. Indeed he found what he called the "de Sitter effect," which was the fact that the red shift of the light coming from a galaxy increases with the galaxy's distance from us. This is now called "Hubble's Law." Perhaps it should be called the "Hubble–de Sitter Law."

After Hubble's work came out, Einstein abandoned the cosmological constant of his theory of relativity. There was no need for it. But one can wonder why Einstein did not discover Friedmann's solutions himself and make de Sitter's prediction for the more general case of an expanding universe. By the 1920s, even though Einstein was still a towering figure in physics, one can see the center of the field gradually shifting away from him to a new and younger generation of physicists: the generation of the quantum theory.

6

The Stranger Story of the Quantum

In 1913 a distinguished group of German scientists, including Max Planck, wrote a letter of recommendation for Einstein to the Prussian Academy of Sciences, of which they were members. Einstein was only 34, but his reputation was already such that they thought that he should be elected to their illustrious society in Berlin. The final paragraph of this letter is a gem. It reads: "In sum, one can say that there is hardly one among the great problems, in which modern physics is so rich, which Einstein has not made some remarkable contribution. That he may sometimes have missed the target in his speculations as, for example, in his hypothesis of light quanta cannot really be held against him, for it is not possible to introduce really new ideas, even in the most exact sciences, without sometimes taking a risk."

In short, Planck, one of the authors of this remarkable document, was saying even in 1913 that the idea of light quanta "missed the target" and should not be held against Einstein. Planck, who had devised the idea of quanta, still was unable to grasp the significance of his own creation.

When we left quantum physics it was 1906, and Einstein was still the dominant figure in it. He had just published his paper about how solids absorb heat. Einstein did publish some work on quantum physics between 1906 and 1916. But his next important work was published in 1916. It led a half century later to the development of the laser. That Einstein could do this work at the same time he was developing general relativity demonstrates his almost incredible intellectual power at this time.

By 1916 there was still no theory from which one could derive the Planck blackbody law. This would not come until quantum mechanics was created a decade later. We have just seen that as late as 1913 Planck was referring to Einstein's quantum as if it were something that might be held against him. Planck himself had only recently abandoned his futile attempt to derive his formula from classical physics. In his 1916 work, Einstein once again proceeded in a "heuristic" fashion—assuming Planck's formula and seeing what would be needed to derive it.

For the purposes of his 1916 argument, he imagined an idealized atom that could have only two states of energy. It had a state of least energy, usually called the "ground state," and a state with a higher energy called an "excited state." Suppose that a collection of these atoms found themselves in a bath of radiation, at some temperature, perhaps different from the temperature of the atoms. Einstein studied the processes by which the atoms and the radiation could then reach a common temperature. He argued that three things can happen. First, a photon with just the right energy can be absorbed and cause an atom in its ground state to be energized into its excited state. Second, an atom in its excited state can make a spontaneous transition back to its gound state, emitting a photon in the process. This is called "spontaneous emission." Third, an atom in its excited state can be induced, or stimulated, to return to its ground state by the presence of light quanta with just the right energy. This is called "stimulated emission," since it takes place only if there are other light quanta around. When the atom is induced to return to its ground state this way, it also emits an additional light quantum. Einstein showed that the only way in which one could derive Planck's formula for radiation was if there was this process of stimulated emission along with the others. If Planck's formula was right, there had to be stimulated emission.

But suppose one encloses these atoms within a box that can contain all of the radiation in the hypothetical "bath." Let us also suppose that prior to our experiment we have been able to energize a bunch of these atoms into their excited state. To do this, we imagine having introduced a beam of radiation of just the right frequency to cause transitions of the atoms from their ground state to their excited state—something called "optical pumping." The excited atoms will then begin spontaneously to emit photons that have the same frequency as those with which the atoms were excited. These photons cannot escape; they are trapped in the box. But they are at just the right energy to cause stimulated emission. Consequently, these newly created photons can cause even further stimulated emissions, producing even more photons that can cause still more stimulated emissions. Through this "cascade" effect the signal that originally pumped up the atoms into their excited states will be vastly amplified. This in fact is the principle of the maser and the laser.

The maser, which stands for Microwave Amplification by Stimulated Emission of Radiation, was first constructed only in the early 1950s, some four decades after Einstein's paper. It turned out that using microwaves, which have wavelengths of about a centimeter, was easier for this purpose than using visible light to excite the molecules in a maser. The molecule used in the first maser experiments was ammonia, which consists of one nitrogen atom and three hydrogen atoms. A few years later, the first laser, which stands for Light Amplification by Stimulated Emission of Radiation, was made. Einstein's 1916 paper was at the basis of all of it.

For a physicist, however, the real interest in the quantum theory is not so much in these applications as in what the theory reveals about nature. We shall describe enough of it here so that we can understand Einstein's bizarre—some would say tragic—relationship to it. In one way or another, this problem was to occupy the final 30 years of Einstein's life. We will begin our story with the discovery of the atomic nucleus by the great New Zealand-born experimental physicist Ernest Rutherford. In 1909, Rutherford, then a professor at Manchester University in England, had a student named Ernest Marsden who was looking for a problem on which to work. Rutherford suggested allowing alpha particles (which we now know are the nuclei of helium atoms), which were produced during the decay of heavy radioactive elements like radium, to hit a thin foil of gold. We call this a "scattering" experiment— the scattering of alpha particles by gold. At the time of this experiment there existed a widely accepted picture of the atom that had been invented by the British physicist J. J. Thomson, the discoverer of the electron. In Thomson's model the atom resembled a raisin pudding, in which the positive charge was the pudding and the electrons, whose collective negative charge balanced the positive charge of the atom, were strewn about like the raisins. According to this model the alpha particles striking the gold foil should pass through the gold atoms in the foil like bullets through pudding. This is what Rutherford thought would happen. Nonetheless, he advised Marsden and Hans Geiger—who

In 1909 physicist Ernest Rutherford discovered the atomic nucleus. In the 1930s—before fission—Rutherford and Einstein shared the idea that nuclear energy would never have any practical use.

later invented the counter we still use to detect and measure radiation, and who was working with Marsden—to keep an eye out for possible collisions in which an alpha particle did not pass straight through the foil but was deflected at a large angle. Much to everyone's astonishment, there were some deflections. Rutherford later called this "quite the most incredible event that has ever happened to me in my life. It was almost as incredible as if you fired a 15-inch shell at a piece of tissue paper and it came back and hit you." There was something hard in the interior of the atom. Rutherford and his students had discovered the atomic nucleus.

The next player in the game was Niels Bohr. In 1911 he received his Ph.D. at the university of Copenhagen and then won a traveling fellowship that allowed him to study in England. Bohr decided to go to Rutherford's lab in Manchester. It was a wonderful, though unlikely, choice. It was unlikely because on the surface the two men had totally different personalities. Rutherford was a booming extrovert whose voice could be heard all over the laboratory. Bohr was at the time an extremely shy postgraduate student. In later life he became a self-confident man of the world who dealt routinely with presidents, prime ministers, kings, and captains of industry; he had no problem in raising money for the things he believed in, such as his Institute for Theoretical Physics in Copenhagen. By comparison, it is impossible to imagine Einstein writing grant proposals to finance an institute or even directing an institute. In 1912 Bohr returned to Copenhagen, and during the next year he created the atomic model that really began the modern atomic age.

Through his contact with Rutherford, Bohr was convinced that the atom consisted of a minuscule positively charged nucleus surrounded by electrons moving in orbits around the nucleus like planets around the Sun. But he also realized that this simple picture had something very wrong with it. An accelerating charge emits radiation and therefore loses energy. Consequently, an electron in one of these orbits of Bohr's atom would lose energy and begin falling into the nucleus. Matter would be unstable. But apart from this, the model would provide no way in which to explain the beautiful spectra of light given off when gases of atoms are heated or otherwise excited. When this is done, the atom of each chemical element gives off light in a pattern of spectral lines that is as distinctive as a fingerprint. If electrons simply spiraled into the nucleus, as they would in a classical physics model of the atom, the light they would give off would be a jumble of frequencies with no particular meaning or order. Getting spectral patterns out of this model would be like dropping a grand piano out of a window and expecting it to play Beethoven's *Moonlight* Sonata when it hit the sidewalk. A radical change in the classical atomic model was needed. Bohr, who was 27 when he began this work, made it.

Bohr realized that so long as the electrons in an atom obeyed the classical laws of motion, they could occupy any orbit around the nucleus with any energy. Light of all frequencies would be emitted by the electrons circulating in these orbits in a total jumble. In order to account for the observed spectra, Bohr assumed an atom's electrons could orbit around the nucleus only in certain *allowed* orbits. These came to be called the "Bohr orbits," and their elliptical shapes have become part of the symbol that is now commonly used to depict the atom. Each Bohr orbit is characterized by a specific energy. The Bohr orbit with the lowest energy is called the ground state. If an electron is stimulated into one of its excited states it will work its way back to the ground state by jumping from one allowed orbit to another. If it jumps from an orbit with an energy E to an orbit with a smaller energy E', it will emit a photon with an energy given by $h\nu = E - E'$. Here ν is the frequency of the light and h is Planck's constant. Since there is no lower energy than that of the ground state, an electron in that state cannot lose any more energy by radiation once it gets there. Therefore, the ground state is perfectly stable. What persuaded people that Bohr's model of the atom contained a large portion of the truth was Bohr's ability to use it to account for the spectral pattern characteristic of hydrogen, the simplest known atom, whose nucleus consists of only a proton with a single electron orbiting around it. When Einstein heard about Bohr's work, he pronounced it one of the greatest discoveries of 20th-century physics.

Bohr returned the compliment in January 1920, when he nominated Einstein as a foreign member of the Danish Academy of Science. Although the two men had never met, before the year was out they would have not one, but two, opportunities to get together. In April Bohr visited Berlin to give a lecture, and afterward Einstein wrote, "Not often in life has a person, by his mere presence, given me such joy as you did."

Bohr and Einstein met again four months later. Einstein had gone to Norway, and on his way back to Berlin he stopped off in Copenhagen. Writing to Lorentz, he reported that "the trip to Kristiana [Oslo] was really beautiful, the most beautiful were the hours I spent with Bohr in Copenhagen."

Einstein and Bohr each learned they had won the Nobel Prize on the same day, November 11, 1922. Einstein won the physics prize for 1921 (the awarding of the prize had been postponed one year), and Bohr for 1922. Einstein was not able to attend the prize ceremony in Stockholm, because he and his wife were on a trip to Japan, but to make up for his absence, he lectured in Sweden the following year. On his way back, he again visited Bohr in Copenhagen.

During the next decade a great many physicists devoted themselves to working out the details of Bohr's theory. The theory of special relativity was also applied, which led to even more complicated orbits that explained some of the

Einstein relaxing with the Dutch physicist Niels Bohr, 1927. Although they disagreed about the quantum theory, Einstein and Bohr were friends for life.

fine details in observed atomic spectra. But it also became clear that there were things that the Bohr theory could not account for at all. It could not, for example, explain the spectra of atoms that contained more than one electron. The spectrum of helium—an atom with only two electrons—was a challenge that the Bohr theory was never able to master. And even for hydrogen, although Bohr's model of the atom accounted very well for the positions of its spectral lines, it could not account for their relative brightness—why was one line more intense than another? All of the successes and failures of the Bohr theory fell under the umbrella of what came to be known as the "old quantum theory," whose correct features later became incorporated into what is now known simply as the "quantum theory."

The first step to the quantum theory came from a very unlikely source: the Ph.D. thesis of a 31-year-old French nobleman named Louis de Broglie. The de Broglies were an old and wealthy French family. Louis's older brother Maurice became fascinated by physics while serving in the French navy. When he proposed resigning his commission to do research, his family was scandalized. It was finally decided that the only acceptable thing to do was to create a private laboratory for him in the family mansion in Paris. Maurice de Broglie became a first-rate X-ray spectroscopist, which inspired his younger brother Louis to go into physics as well. Louis became interested in the theory of radiation and wrote papers on it prior to writing his Ph.D. thesis. In the fall of 1923 he made, for purely speculative reasons (since there was no experimental evidence to support it), the proposal that the relation that connects momentum p to the energy $E = h\nu$ of a light quantum, $p = h\nu/c$, should apply to particles like electrons as well as to light! A particle with a momentum p should, De Broglie proposed, have some sort of wave associated with it with a frequency determined by its momentum. In other words, an electron should have a wave nature as well as a particle nature. This was the flip side of the idea that light had a particle as well as a wave nature. It was a completely radical departure from classical physics—a much bolder step than relativity had been.

In 1923, De Broglie submitted this idea to his thesis advisor, Paul Langevin, who did not quite know what to make of it and who sent a copy to Einstein. Einstein was immediately taken by the bold idea of this unknown physicist. What had impressed Einstein about de Broglie's work, and why was he able to distinguish de Broglie's thesis from crank physics—which, at first glance, it resembles? (See sidebar on next page.)

As exciting as they were, de Broglie waves created as many puzzles as they solved. Most significant of these was the question of what they were. The first idea—certainly

text continues on page 138

HOW TO DETECT CRANK PHYSICS

How can we distinguish an idea like that of de Broglie's, which looks crazy, from a really crank idea?

This is an important point, and if you absorb its lessons, you too may be able to distinguish real physics from crank physics.

In the first place, de Broglie's idea did not contradict anything that was already known. We don't see ordinary matter exhibiting a wave nature, and de Broglie's notion conformed to this. To see that it did, we note that for the light quantum we have the relation $p = h\nu/c = h/\lambda$, where p is the momentum and λ is the wave length of the light and we have used the relation $\lambda\nu = c$. It is this relationship that de Broglie had proposed to generalize to material particles. If such a particle has a momentum p, then the de Broglie wave length of that particle is defined to be $\lambda = h/p$. For a nonrelativistic particle, the momentum p is given in terms of its speed v and mass m, by the equation $p = mv$. Accordingly, we have the de Broglie wave length given by $\lambda = h/mv$. The size of this wave length therefore depends then on the speed of the particle and its mass. Let us take as an example an electron moving at one hundredth of the speed of light. Its rest mass is 9.1×10^{-31} kilograms—a minuscule mass compared to the mass of anything we deal with in daily life. The de Broglie wave length of this electron turns out to be about 10^{-10} meters—the size of an average atom. But according to de Broglie's formula, the wavelength of a kilogram-like mass moving at the same speed would be some 10^{31} times smaller than that of our electron. The wave nature of such an object would be totally unobservable! You couldn't construct, for example, an ordinary optical diffraction grating that would be sensitive to such tiny effects. That is why we cannot dismiss de Broglie's idea—precisely because it does not disagree with our daily experience.

The second reason why Einstein and others took de Broglie's idea seriously was much more significant. It appeared to supply a deeper

continues on page 136

text continued from page 135

understanding of the orbits of the electrons in Bohr's model of the atom. Bohr had assumed the existence of such orbits. But if the electron really did have a wave nature, it seemed possible to justify this assumption. For an electron to be in such an orbit, its associated wave would have to fit exactly around the nucleus of the atom. But the only way in which such a wave—with its troughs and crests—could fit around the nucleus would be if the circumference of the orbit was precisely a whole integer number of wavelengths. One could have one complete wave, or two complete waves, and so on, but not, say, a half a wave that would not fit the orbit. This integer condition sufficed to allow one to derive the positions of the allowed Bohr orbits of hydrogen—their distance from the nucleus. That is what caught everyone's attention.

Finally, de Broglie's hypothesis permitted one to make a prediction that could be tested by experiment. Indeed, like the predictions of Einstein's relativity theory, it *cried out* to be tested by experiment—namely, what the wavelength of an electron of a given momentum would be. This is also a very important point. Crank physics almost never makes a real, testable prediction. The person who comes to you with a plan for a perpetual motion machine—something that violates all the known laws of thermodynamics—is hardly presenting you with something that is testable. Even if you could build it, how do you know it will run forever? But the existence of the de Broglie waves was testable, and it was testable with experiments that could be and were done with the technology available in the mid-1920s. The test was suggested by de Broglie himself, and was taken up by Einstein. De Broglie realized that since an electron with a moderate speed had a wave length that was about the size of an atom, a beam of such electrons directed onto a crystalline solid should show the kind of interference effects that light shows when it impinges on a grating. One should find a pattern of light and dark fringes of the kind that Thomas Young first observed at the beginning of the 19th century when he convinced his contemporaries that light was a wave phenomenon! De Broglie published his idea in 1923. In 1927, it was tested in independent experiments done in the United States by C. J. Davisson and L. H. Germer, and in Scotland by G. P. Thomson (the son of James J. Thomson). These experiments showed that de Broglie had been right—the electron did have a wave nature. In 1929 Prince Louis de Broglie was awarded the Nobel Prize in Physics for his Ph.D. thesis.

Einstein's idea—was that de Broglie's waves were real waves in space. Einstein believed that these waves guided the electron along like some sort of radar. In the next few years this picture, at least in this relatively simple form, turned out to be impossible.

The two men most responsible for showing that it was impossible—and for starting the revolution in quantum theory—were Werner Heisenberg and Erwin Schrödinger. Although the work of Schrödinger was done in 1926, a year later than the work of Heisenberg, we will begin with Schrödinger's work since it follows directly from the concept of the de Broglie waves. It is also one of the rare examples of truly revolutionary work in theoretical physics done by someone who was nearly 40—a very advanced age for novel work in this field—and Einstein initially embraced it as work of "real genius." Remarkably, a few years before 1926, Schrödinger, who had not done anything of major importance in physics until then, had decided to give up physics and teach philosophy instead. He would have done so, except that the teaching job he was counting on fell through. So he returned to physics, and as he later noted, "to my astonishment something occasionally emerged from it." What emerged in 1926 was a modification of the quantum theory—or at least one version of it. In reaching his version of the theory, Schrödinger's first step was to produce the equation that has carried his name ever since—the Schrödinger equation. It is to quantum physics what Newton's law is to classical mechanics. It is not really correct to say that Schrödinger "derived" this equation. You cannot derive quantum theory from classical physics. At some point you have to make a logical leap.

Austrian physicist Erwin Schrödinger. Einstein was deeply impressed by Schrödinger's discovery of his wave equation.

With Schrödinger's equation you can solve the problem of an electron orbiting around a proton under the influence of the electrical force of attraction between the positively charged nucleus of the atom and the negatively charged electron, as in the case of the hydrogen atom. Schrödinger discovered that the equation had solutions for only certain allowed energies of the electron, and that these energies were precisely the energy levels Bohr had found. One could plot Schrödinger's solutions, and one then could see that where the waves had large amplitudes was just at the positions of the Bohr orbits. All of this was wonderful, and Einstein was initially full of enthusiasm for it.

However, his enthusiasm was not very long-lived. Einstein's disenchantment with Schrödinger's work had to do with how a Schrödinger wave can evolve in time. One can imagine taking such a wave and compressing it to atomic dimensions. Under these conditions, it turns out that the wave will begin to spread. If it corresponds to a particle with the mass of the electron, it will within a few days have spread so far that it covers the entire solar system! But any electron actually observed is a tiny, localized object, and not some glutinous monster spread out all over space. What, then, do the Schrödinger waves really mean?

The answer was given in June 1926 by the German physicist Max Born. Born was born in 1882, making him five years older than Schrödinger and three years younger than Einstein. Of the three, it was only Born who really accepted the quantum theory. He, Einstein, and Mrs. Born conducted a remarkable three-way correspondence for 40 years. Throughout much of this period, Born kept trying to get Einstein to accept the quantum theory, and in his letters Einstein explained why he could not.

What Born proposed was that the de Broglie-Schrödinger waves were not ordinary waves, but rather waves of *probability*. Once one accepts this, the apparent paradox of the glutinous electron disappears. The spreading of the de Broglie-Schrödinger wave means that within a short time there will be an extremely minute probability of finding the electron far from its initial location. Where, in space, the wave function is large, the electron will most likely be found. Similarly, a large wave function for the electron of hydrogen at the location of the Bohr orbits is where one is most likely—although not certain—to find the electron. It was this probability aspect of Bohr's proposal that Einstein could not stomach.

The only thing we can predict is where a particle is most likely to be. Einstein reacted against this concept from the beginning. In December 1926 he wrote to Born, "Quantum mechanics is certainly imposing. But an inner voice tells me that it is not yet the real thing. The theory says a lot, but does not really bring us any closer to the secret of the 'old one' [Einstein's affectionate name for God]. I at any rate, am convinced that *He* is not playing at dice."

After 1926, Niels Bohr became the intellectual conscience of the quantum theory—defending it against the skepticism of Einstein. Bohr was only six years younger than Einstein, but in physics he seemed to belong to another generation. He found the quantum theory—and most physicists agree—to be the most profound scientific theory ever created. Under Bohr's tutelage and relentless criticism Heisenberg produced his famous principles of uncertainty, of which the most understandable is the principle that links the position and momentum of a subatomic particle such as an electron. In essence, this principle says that if you design an experiment that measures the position of a particle perfectly then the experiment will not be able to measure the momentum of the particle at all. Indeed, if the momentum of the particle is not measured, we do not even have the right, according to quantum theory, to assume that it exists. Conversely, if we design an experiment that exactly measures the momentum of a particle, that same experiment can tell us nothing about the position of the particle. From the viewpoint of quantum theory, the particle has no position. The uncertainty principle therefore tells us what we can and cannot learn about both quantities in the same experiment—in contrast to most experiments, which tell us about either of these quantities with only limited precision.

Heisenberg spelled out these ideas in 1927, and Bohr used them to create what he called the "principle of complementarity." Bohr noted that the uncertainty principles make it impossible to design an experiment that simultaneously exhibits both the particle and the wave nature of an object such as the electron or the photon. Thus, while the electron will in some experiments act like a particle and in others like a wave, Bohr's principle assures us that these two facets of its behavior will never come into conflict with each other. It has even been suggested that the electron be called a "wavicle" to commemorate its double nature.

Heisenberg's uncertainty principles gave Einstein something to sink his teeth into. He decided to try to show that they were wrong. To this end, in what was perhaps a throwback to his days in the Swiss patent office, he invented ingenious imaginary devices that seemed to be able to measure simultaneously both position and momentum, or energy and time (which were the subjects of another of Heisenberg's principles). He made ingenious sketches of these devices and threw them out as challenges to his colleagues in quantum physics at the Solvay Conferences. These meetings were held in Brussels and attended by the greatest physicists of the day.

The fifth Solvay Conference was held for six days in October 1927. The three founding quantum physicists— Planck, Einstein, and for the first time, Bohr—were there, as well as the younger workers—including de Broglie, Heisenberg, and Schrödinger. Lorentz chaired the meeting. Einstein took the role of critic. In informal discussions, Einstein presented several imaginary devices that purported

to show that the quantum theory did not work. By carefully considering these devices Bohr showed that the theory
did in fact work.

But the most extraordinary encounter took place at the
Solvay Conference of 1930. For that occasion Einstein had
cooked up a device that seemed to refute Heisenberg's principle of uncertainty with regard to energy and time. It consisted of a box with a hole in its wall that can be opened by
a shutter. The timing of the opening is controlled by a
clock. Inside the box is radiation. The box is weighed on a
scale on which the box sits. The clock records the time and
the shutter is opened. Out flies a photon. The shutter is
instantly closed and the box weighed again. By comparing
the two weights, we know how much energy the photon
took off from the box, and we also seem to know the time.
We seem to have constructed a device that violates the
uncertainty principle between energy and time.

When he first saw Einstein's device, Bohr was both baf-
fled and extremely distressed. He spent what one gathers

*The delegates to the
Sixth Solvay Conference,
1930. Einstein is seated
in the front row, fifth
from right.*

must have been a sleepless night trying to save Heisenberg's theory. By the next morning he had the solution. There is an uncertainty in the measurement of the weight of the box, since if we imagine that we measure it by having a pointer point to some number on a scale, there is, according to Heisenberg, an uncertainty in the position of the pointer. To determine the position of the pointer exactly, we have to impart some momentum to the scale. But the scale moves in the gravitational field of the earth, as we remember, and since the time measured by a clock depends on where it is in a gravitational field—as Einstein had stated in his principle of equivalence—there will be an uncertainty in the knowledge of when the shutter door opened. If one works this out in detail, it will be found to agree perfectly with Heisenberg's uncertainty principle. Einstein's feelings about the quantum theory were so strong that he had ignored his own greatest discovery in trying to refute it.

Einstein lived in this simple house at 112 Mercer Street in Princeton, New Jersey, from 1935 until his death in 1955.

112 Mercer Street

The house in which Einstein lived from 1935 until his death in 1955 was at 112 Mercer Street in Princeton, New Jersey. Some two miles from the Institute for Advanced Study, to which Einstein was appointed in 1932, it is now occupied by a physicist at the Institute and his family. It is a simple, cottagelike home. There is no plaque at the front indicating that Einstein ever lived there.

If the Nazis had not come to power in Germany, it is very unlikely that Einstein would have left that country and come to Princeton. He was genuinely contented in Berlin. He had a superb job, surrounded by brilliant and appreciative colleagues and students. He even gave a seminar in his beloved statistical mechanics. A few of the people who took it are still alive and remember it as one of the great intellectual experiences of their lives. In the summer of 1929 Einstein bought a small plot of land in the village of Caputh, near Berlin. On it, he built a summer house for his family. It was close to the Havel River. On his 50th birthday his friends presented him with a sailboat and he spent a great deal of his time sailing on the river by himself. It was an ideal place to think.

But even as early as 1920 Einstein had already become a target for the anti-Semitism that was growing in Germany. He was a perfect target. He had been a pacifist during the war. Even his German citizenship was suspect. His face was known everywhere, and he had invented a theory that defied common sense and made many people—including some of the older generation of physicists—extremely uncomfortable. In February 1920 Einstein gave a public lecture at the University of Berlin at which a small riot broke out. It was never fully explained, but Einstein felt that it had hints of anti-Semitism in it.

By later that year, however, there was no doubt about the mood toward Jews in Germany. An anti-Einstein league was formed, and in late August it sponsored a rally in Berlin's largest concert hall. Einstein attended. He was not amused. Swastikas and anti-Semitic pamphlets were for sale. Philipp Lenard, who had won the Nobel Prize in physics in 1905 for his work on electrons, had already begun his attempt to discredit Einstein. Lenard was an early and very enthusiastic Nazi. He unearthed two non-Jewish German scientists, one long dead and one who died in World War I, whom he said should really be credited with relativity. The first was a German mathematician and surveyor named Johann Georg von Soldner, who in 1801 had suggested that gravity might bend light. This is not very surprising, since at that time it was still possible to believe that light was a particle phenomenon and that its particles had mass. In Newton's law this mass cancels out so we do not have to know it. Indeed, if you perform the calculation of the path of the light ray, you will be led to the bending that is given by the Principle of Equivalence alone. The bending has nothing to do with the alteration of the geometry of space-time in Einstein's General Theory of Relativity.

The second of Lenard's candidates for the creation of relativity was a promising Austrian physicist named Friedrich Hasenhohrl, who had been Schrödinger's favorite teacher at the University of Vienna. Hasenhohrl had done some research on radiation in a cavity prior to Einstein's 1905 paper, and he had noted that the energy of this radiation might be related to a mass through the equation $E = mc^2$. Lenard seized on this fact to show that Einstein had done nothing original. Since Hasenhohrl was dead, he was conveniently unavailable for comment. Lenard might have had a better case had he chosen Lorentz, since the transformations that Einstein derived from the Special Theory of Relativity were first written down by Lorentz. But Lorentz, who died in 1928, was still very much alive and was one of Einstein's greatest admirers—a feeling that was mutual.

Einstein reacted to the August meeting of the anti-Einstein league, and to Lenard, who was a key figure in it, in a humanly understandable but very uncharacteristic way: he lost his temper, and he did so publicly, in a local newspaper. This prompted an anxious letter from Mrs. Born in which she wrote, "We are extremely sorry to hear about the unpleasant rows that are worrying you. You must have suffered very much from them, for otherwise you would not have allowed yourself to be goaded into that rather unfortunate reply in the newspapers. Those who know you are sad and suffer with you, because they can see that you have taken this infamous mischief-making <u>very</u> much to heart. Those who do not know you get a false picture of you. That hurts too...." Interestingly, Mrs. Born then went on to urge Einstein not to leave Germany, implying that the "mischief" to which she referred was the work of some lunatic fringe not worthy of Einstein's attention. Einstein was duly embarrassed, and in a letter of reply, asked the Borns not to "be too hard on me. Everyone has to sacrifice on the altar of stupidity from time to time, to please the Deity and the human race. And this I have done thoroughly with my article....In the first moment of attack I probably thought of flight. But soon my insight and the phlegm returned. Today I think only of buying a sailing boat and a

country cottage close to water. Somewhere near Berlin...."
But by the time, nine years later, that he realized this dream
in Caputh, the Nazis were really on the rise, and the handwriting for Einstein in Germany was on the wall.

As we have learned, after his earliest childhood Einstein
never practiced a formal religion, although he readily
acknowledged his Jewishness. But in 1924 he actually joined
a temple. It was not that his views about religion had
changed, but rather that he wanted to show solidarity with
his people at a time when they were under increasing attack.
One of the most moving photographs of Einstein was taken
in a Berlin synagogue in 1930. In it he is shown with his
violin, wearing the traditional Jewish skullcap. He was about
to play in a benefit concert to raise money to help his fellow
Jews. In the background one sees the faces of the congrega-
tion. We know, although they did not, what is going to happen to those of them who remained in Germany once the
Holocaust began. Einstein also developed an interest in
Zionism, the movement to establish a Jewish homeland in
what was then called Palestine (now Israel). This was, again,
not because he had changed his mind about nations. He
never really felt himself to be the citizen of any country—
although in his lifetime he had been the citizen of three. But
he saw that a homeland in Palestine would be a way to save
the Jews of Europe. He was also very interested in helping to
found a university in that homeland, and he ultimately did
contribute to the development of the Hebrew University in
Jerusalem. In 1952, four years after the founding of the state
of Israel, Einstein was asked to be the second president of
Israel when its first president, Chaim Weizmann, died. He
turned the job down partly for reasons of health and partly
because he did not think himself suitable by temperament to
exercise what he called in his letter of refusal "official functions."

By the end of 1931 Einstein had decided, at least pri-
vately, that he was going to leave Germany. During the previous winter, he had visited the California Institute of

Technology in Pasadena, and while there he had met Albert
Michelson and Edwin Hubble. Michelson had still not fully
reconciled himself to relativity and the loss of the ether theory. But Einstein's meeting with Hubble persuaded him to
drop the cosmological constant from his 1917 equations for
the theory of general relativity. In the winter of 1932
Einstein made a second visit to Cal Tech. By this time it
had been suggested that he might like to come to the
Institute permanently, or at least as a long-term visitor. The
amount of his salary had even been discussed. But during
this second visit Einstein had an encounter with an
American educator named Abraham Flexner that eventually
changed his mind.

In 1929, just before the crash of the stock market,
Louis Bamberger and his sister, Mrs. Felix Fuld, the owners
of the R. H. Macy & Company department store, decided
to sell the store. They invested $5 million of the proceeds in
education and sought out Flexner, who had written books
about how to reform higher education, for advice. Flexner
did have an idea. It was to create an institution where creative scholarship could take place at the most advanced

*Einstein with the physics
department faculty and
graduate students of the
California Institute of
Technology, 1932.
Einstein declined an offer
to join Cal Tech's faculty
and instead accepted a
position at the Institute
for Advanced Study in
Princeton, New Jersey.*

level. Flexner called it an Institute for Advanced Study. In a memorandum he wrote for Bamberger and Fuld, he said that this institute "should be small, that its staff and students or scholars should be few, that members of the teaching staff, should freely participate in decisions involving the character, quality, and direction of its activities, that its subjects should be fundamental in character, and that it should develop gradually." To an academic, all of this sounds like heaven on Earth.

Flexner had decided that the first appointments to the planned institute should be in mathematics and theoretical physics, since neither of these disciplines needed funding for laboratories. He may also have known that it is easier for people working in these fields to agree on who is really outstanding than it is for people working in the social sciences or humanities. Flexner went to the California Institute of Technology to seek the advice of its president, Robert Millikan. Millikan, it appears, suggested that Flexner talk to Einstein, not thinking that Flexner might eventually try to lure Einstein away from Cal Tech. The two men met and talked, and they agreed to meet again in England, where Einstein was to visit Oxford in the spring of 1932. At Oxford they again discussed the planned Institute. But this time Flexner suggested that Einstein might be interested in becoming its first physicist. Nothing was decided, but at a third meeting, in Berlin, after Einstein's return to Germany, Einstein decided to come.

Einstein proposed for himself an annual salary of $3,000. It is not clear how he arrived at this figure. He even asked Flexner if he could live on less. Flexner must have realized that economics was not Einstein's strong suit, and the discussion was turned over to Mrs. Einstein. It was agreed that Einstein would be paid a salary of $16,000 a year—a very high academic salary for those days. Even so, Einstein still did not consider this arrangement to be permanent; he requested only a five-month leave of absence from his job in Berlin, saying that he would be back. But by the end of 1932, when he finally left Caputh, he told his wife to take a good look at the house. When she asked why, he told her it was because she would never see it again. He was right. She died in Princeton in 1936, and Einstein never again set foot in Germany.

In the spring of 1933 his home in Caputh was raided by an armed mob searching, they said, for "weapons." But by this time Einstein and his wife were on the high seas bound for Belgium, where they set up temporary residence in the seaside resort of Le Cocque. Thus Einstein did not have to witness the public burning of his writings on relativity, along with other books regarded as being "Bolshevistic," that took place about this time in front of the Berlin State Opera House. Since no location in Belgium is more than a few hours drive from the German border, there was serious concern that Einstein might be kidnapped or assassinated. He was assigned security guards and the people of Le Cocque were told to say nothing about him. Philipp Frank often used to tell the story of how he broke through this "wall" of security. Frank happened to be in Belgium and heard that Einstein was staying somewhere in the region of Le Cocque. Not knowing anything about the security measures, Frank went there and innocently asked various locals how to find Einstein. They told him! But when he went to Einstein's house he was in for a bit of a surprise. No sooner did he appear than he was seized by two security men. He was released only when Mrs. Einstein recognized him.

On September 9, Einstein left Le Cocque for England, and there, on October 7, boarded the ocean liner *Westmoreland*. Elsa, his secretary Helen Dukas, and his assistant Walther Mayer were already on board. Ten days later they were in the United States. They were driven to Princeton, where rooms had been reserved for them at a local inn. Shortly thereafter, the Einsteins and Miss Dukas moved into a rented house. They bought 112 Mercer Street—paying for it in cash—two years later. The Institute did not at that time have its own quarters. But the president of Princeton University turned over to it part of Fine Hall, which housed the mathematics department. Here Einstein had his office until 1940, when the Institute constructed its own campus outside Princeton. A visitor to Fine Hall can still see one memento from those early days. In 1925 an American physicist named Dayton Miller made a positive claim that he had actually been able to measure the effect of Michelson's beloved ether on the motion of light—a proof that had eluded Michelson himself. That would, of course, have finished the theory of relativity. When Einstein, still in Germany, heard rumors of this in fact incorrect result, he said, "God is subtle but not malicious." The Princeton mathematician Oswald Veblen, who became Einstein's first colleague at the Institute, heard this story in 1930 and asked Einstein's permission to have the German version of this sentence—"Raffiniert ist der Herr Gott, aber boshaft ist er nicht"—chiseled over a fireplace in a room in Fine Hall. It is still there, although the Princeton mathematics depart-ment has moved to other quarters.

It is probably fair to say that Einstein was never really entirely at home in the United States. When he came here he was in his early 50s. Though he knew some English and spoke some French, he was not really a linguist. But in mid-dle age he had to learn to navigate in English. His closest associates in the United States were mainly German-speaking. German remained the language of Einstein's household and was the language in which he continued to conduct most of his enormous correspondence.

One person to whom he wrote regularly was the queen of Belgium. In November 1933, not long after he moved to Princeton, he wrote her, "Since I left Belgium I have been the recipient of many kindnesses, both direct and indirect. Insofar as possible I have taken to heart the wise counseling of those who urged me to observe silence in political and public affairs, not from fear for myself, but because I saw no opportunity for doing any good." He continued, "Princeton is a wonderful little spot, a quaint and ceremonious village of puny demigods on stilts. Yet by ignoring certain social conventions, I have been able to create for myself an atmosphere conducive to study and free from distraction." His sense of isolation, largely self-imposed, increased, and a year later he wrote to the queen that "Among my

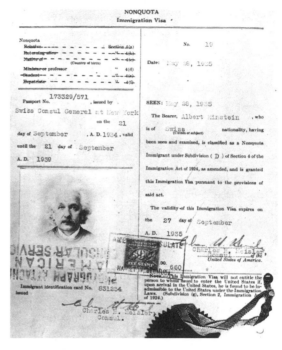

When Einstein decided in 1935 to seek U.S. citizenship, immigration laws required him to leave the United States and then reenter on this immigrant visa. He spent nine days in Bermuda with his wife, stepdaughter, and secretary.

European friends I am now called 'the Great Stone Face' a title I well deserve for having been so completely silent. The gloomy and evil events in Europe have paralyzed me to such an extent that words of a personal nature do not seem able to flow any more from my pen. Thus I have locked myself into quite hopeless scientific problems—more so since, as an elderly man, I have remained estranged from the society here."

We will find out more about the "quite hopeless scientific problems" Einstein was "locked into" in the next chapter; here I only want to make clear how far out of the mainstream in physics Einstein had gotten. This is also important in understanding Einstein's role in the development of the atomic bomb. It will become clear that from a technical viewpoint he had no role in this project, something that is often misunderstood.

By the time Einstein came to Princeton he was no longer claiming that the quantum theory was inconsistent. Perhaps his encounters with Bohr had persuaded him of that. But he was claiming that the theory was incomplete—

that it was incapable of describing large portions of reality. A quantum theorist would reply that those portions of "reality" that the theory cannot describe do not really exist. The issue can be resolved only if someone comes up with a better theory than the quantum theory. That is what Einstein tried to do.

What he wanted to do was to find a theory that, like classical physics, did not from its very beginning deal with probabilities. It was his hope that this greater theory would yield the results of the quantum theory not as axioms, or givens, but as deductions. Along the way he expected that particles like the electron and the photon would reveal themselves as solutions to the equations of this greater theory. In addition, Einstein thought that the theory should unite electromagnetism and gravitation within a single unified field, what he called a Unified Field Theory. The quest for the theory was a terribly ambitious program, and most physicists would now say—as many did even at the time— that it was totally misguided. It never went anywhere, which did not especially bother Einstein, who serenely continued to work on it almost literally to his last breath. The intensity of his pursuit of his vision is evident in a letter he wrote to Max Born in 1944:

> We have become Antipodean [totally opposite] in our scientific expectations. You believe in [a] God who plays dice, and I in complete law and order in a world which objectively exists, and which I, in a wildly speculative way, am trying to capture. I firmly *believe,* but I hope that someone will discover a more realistic way, or rather a more tangible basis than it has been my lot to find. Even the great initial success of the quantum theory does not make me believe in the fundamental dice-game, although I am well aware that our younger colleagues interpret this as a consequence of senility. No doubt the day will come when we will see whose instinctive attitude was the correct one.

In the meantime, mainstream physics was making enormous progress, thanks in part to new experimental results and in part to the insights provided by the quantum theory. In the late 1920s Paul Dirac made a marriage of the quantum theory and relativity. He found out how to write the equations of the quantum theory so that they satisfied the requirements of relativity. A child of this marriage was the prediction that antiparticles had to exist. An antiparticle is an object that has the same mass as its corresponding particle, but the opposite electrical charge. That is, if it has an electrical charge, that charge will be of equal magnitude but opposite in sign (positive or negative) to that of the particle. The first antiparticle to be discovered was the anti–electron, or the positron, which was found in cosmic rays by the American physicist Carl Anderson in 1932. Most physicists considered this finding to be a major triumph for the quantum theory.

Quantum mechanics was also used to explain the nature of the chemical bond—how chemical reactions take place, and how atoms are bonded together to make molecules. Its use in this respect was so successful that it inspired Paul Dirac to say that quantum theory already explained "most of physics and all of chemistry." However, although Einstein called Dirac's classic text, *Quantum Mechanics,* the "most logically perfect presentation of the theory," it did not change his mind about its failure to account for what he called "reality"; nor did the triumphs of the theory in the pioneering subject of nuclear physics.

Quantum theory was able to describe nuclear reactions. One of the most striking features of the atomic nucleus, which is the subject of nuclear physics, is that its mass and charge do not match. The simplest atomic nucleus is that of hydrogen, which consists solely of the nuclear particle known as a proton. Consequently, the mass of the hydrogen nucleus is that of the proton. However, helium, the next heaviest element after hydrogen, has a nucleus consisting of two protons, but a nuclear mass equivalent to that of approximately four protons. This means that the nucleus of helium must contain electrically neutral components that are responsible for this difference. Ernest Rutherford, who discovered the proton in 1909, made the natural but incorrect assumption that these electrically neutral components consisted of an electron and a proton stuck together. But in 1932 James Chadwick, one of Rutherford's young associates at Cambridge, discovered that this neutral component was a particle in its own right, known as the neutron, which has slightly more mass than the proton. Since the neutron is electrically neutral it makes an ideal probe of the nucleus. It is not stopped by the electrical repulsion of the protons and can penetrate clear into the nucleus. Soon several groups in various countries began using neutrons to probe a wide variety of materials to see what would happen.

One of the most interesting of these groups was headed by Enrico Fermi in Rome. Fermi made the accidental but extremely important discovery that slow neutrons—neutrons that moved at the speed of particles of a gas at room temperature—were much more effective than fast neutrons in inducing nuclear reactions. In 1935 Fermi and his group shielded a uranium target with aluminum foil to keep out unwanted radiation and bombarded it with slow neutrons. When the nucleus of a uranium atom is broken up by a neutron—an event known as fission—it gives rise to two lighter elements, such as boron and krypton, along with a small number of neutrons. This is a strong, energy-producing reaction, and if Fermi's group had not shielded its uranium target they would certainly have detected it. Instead, nuclear fission was discovered in Germany in 1938 by Otto Hahn and Fritz Strassmann in Berlin, who performed the experiment that produced it, and by Lise Meitner and Otto Frisch, who correctly interpreted the results of this experiment.

At this point in our story it is useful to introduce the curious figure of Leo Szilard. Szilard was born into a well-to-do Jewish family in Budapest, Hungary, in 1898, making him some 20 years younger than Einstein. He began as a student of engineering, but discovered that his interests were really in physics and mathematics. In 1920 Szilard and his younger brother Bela went to Berlin, where Leo soon gave up engineering and enrolled at the university to study physics. He attended the famous Thursday afternoon colloquia at the university, at which Einstein, Planck, and other well-known physicists played a prominent role. Szilard had no lack of nerve. He was highly intelligent, and he therefore felt it quite reasonable to ask Einstein to conduct a seminar for a few students on statistical mechanics. In addition, the Nobel prizewinner Max von Laue, who was the first physicist to visit Einstein in Bern after he had published his theory of relativity, gave Szilard a thesis problem in relativity.

But Szilard soon lost interest in Laue's problem and instead invented one of his own in statistical mechanics. It was a brilliant problem—one of the few things Szilard ever really finished—and after some encouragement from Einstein he gave it to Laue, who accepted it as Szilard's thesis. Szilard tended to flit around problems like a butterfly, and soon he turned his attention to designing a new, noiseless, refrigerator. Einstein collaborated with him on the project, and together they took out several patents.

After a certain amount of wandering, Szilard got a temporary job in Britain. In the fall of 1933, about a year after the discovery of the neutron, Szilard was inspired by reading the text of a speech by Rutherford. Rutherford said that anyone thinking of using the nucleus as a source of energy was talking "moonshine," and Szilard got the idea of a chain reaction. He realized that if a nuclear process—he did not have anything specific in mind, such as fission—produced more neutrons than were needed to initiate it, these new neutrons could initiate further reactions in a runaway—and perhaps explosive—process. Szilard was so taken by this concept, and so concerned that it might fall into the wrong hands, that in 1934 he actually took out a patent on it. Szilard's problem was that he did not know enough about nuclear physics to conceive of fission as the reaction that could produce the extra neutrons needed for his chain reaction. In fairness to him, neither did anyone else, even such highly competent physicists as Bohr and Heisenberg, who were applying quantum mechanics to the nucleus of the atom.

In 1938, when fission was discovered, both Szilard and Fermi were in the United States. Bohr had just made a visit to Princeton and had brought the news that fission had been achieved by Otto Hahn and Lise Meitner and their colleagues in Germany. The announcement created an immense stir in the physics community. Fermi had gotten a position at Columbia University in New York, and Szilard began haunting the place, trying to call the attention of the physicists there to the potential dangers of the fission situation. The urgent question that had to be answered was whether or not additional neutrons were emitted in fission. If so, fission could produce a chain reaction. If not, fission would become merely a fascinating laboratory curiosity. After making a general nuisance of himself, Szilard found a young Columbia physicist named Walter Zinn who was willing to work with him. Together, they observed the extra neutrons coming from the fission reaction. Thus, a chain reaction was possible. For Szilard, this meant that nuclear weapons were a distinct possibility. He also realized that physicists in many other countries, including Germany, were going to make the same discovery. He tried to get his colleagues to impose censorship on themselves so that as little of this information as possible would be disseminated. No one took him seriously—yet.

Part of the reason for this casual attitude was a theoretical discovery that Bohr had made at about the same time. Uranium exists in several "isotopes"—atoms whose nuclei have the same number of protons as the naturally occurring, stable version, but which contain different numbers of neutrons. The most common isotope of uranium is ^{238}U, which has 92 protons and 146 neutrons. But about 0.7 percent of the natural uranium of the kind found in a mine consists of the rare isotope ^{235}U, which has three fewer neutrons in its nucleus. What Bohr realized was that in the experiments that Fermi, Hahn, and others were then conducting it was only this ^{235}U that was being fissioned. It then became clear to Bohr that in order to make anything like a nuclear weapon, one would first have to separate the two isotopes in order to end up with a uranium "fuel" that consisted mostly of ^{235}U. Since the two isotopes have essentially the same chemical behavior and nearly the same mass, Bohr knew that separating them would be very difficult and very expensive. He remarked, "It would take the entire efforts of a country to make a bomb." He was nearly right. Making an atomic bomb turned out to be the most expensive scientific and engineering problem ever undertaken to that time.

During the 1930s Einstein continued to write to the queen of Belgium. His feeling about what was happening in Europe was increasingly despairing. He wrote to the queen in January 1939, "I have been too troubled to write in good cheer. The moral decline we are compelled to witness and the suffering it engenders are so oppressive that one cannot ignore them even for a moment. No matter how deeply one immerses oneself in work, a haunted feeling of inescapable tragedy persists." He had long given up his pacifism of World War I and was now convinced that the only way to stop Hitler was by force.

It is very unlikely that Einstein had followed any of the nuclear physics of the 1930s very closely. It was, after all, applied quantum mechanics. He also felt that the potential use of nuclear energy seemed as remote as "shooting birds in the dark in a country where there are only a few birds." Thanks to Szilard, this perception was about to change.

For several years since coming to the United States, Einstein had been taking his summer vacations on the seashore of Long Island, not far from New York City. In the summer of 1939 he rented a house at Nassau Point, near Peconic, Long Island. Here he could sail and play chamber music with his neighbors and this is where Szilard found him on the July 12 of that year. By that time, Szilard had created a design for a nuclear reactor that used graphite, or purified carbon, to slow the neutrons released by nuclear fission. He was unable to stir up much interest in it, although it later became the basis of the United States's early reactor program. This lack of interest, along with his guess that the Germans were probably doing the same thing—which turned out to be correct—put Szilard into a state of near panic. Szilard had a friend, a fellow Hungarian named Eugene Wigner, who was a nuclear physicist at Princeton. Wigner had also attended Einstein's seminar on statistical mechanics in Berlin. Szilard persuaded Wigner to come to New York to examine his reactor design, and after studying it, Wigner was persuaded that it might work. But what could the two physicists do next?

Wigner remembered that Einstein knew the queen of Belgium. This was relevant, because he knew that it would be easy for the Germans to overrun Belgium and take over the Belgian Congo—one of Belgium's African colonies—which was then the world's largest supplier of uranium. Szilard and Wigner decided that they had to see Einstein on Long Island to persuade him to write to the queen and warn her about the uranium.

Because Szilard did not know how to drive, they set off in Wigner's car. After some confusion about the directions, they eventually found their way to Peconic. Einstein had just come in from sailing when they arrived at his house, but he sat and listened to what they had to say. After Wigner had explained the concept of a chain reaction and how it could be used to make a reactor, or even a bomb, Einstein said in German "Daran habe ich gar nicht gedacht"—"I never thought of that at all." Among his initial reactions, Einstein noted that if one could really use nuclear energy, it would be the first time that mankind had used a source of energy that did not either directly or indirectly come from the Sun. Einstein agreed that the Belgians should be warned, and he dictated a letter to be transmitted to the Belgian ambassador in Washington. The two Hungarians then drove back to New York.

But for Szilard, who was nothing if not obsessive, the meeting with Einstein was not enough. He decided that somehow he had to get to the highest levels of the American government—the President if possible—to warn him of the potential danger in nuclear fission. Through a connection in New York, Szilard got to see Alexander Sachs, an economist who was an adviser to President Franklin D. Roosevelt. Sachs was impressed, and he told Szilard that if he got Einstein to write a letter, he, Sachs, would make sure the President got to see it. This meant another trip to Long Island.

Wigner had gone to California, so Szilard drafted yet another Hungarian physicist, Edward Teller, to drive him back to Einstein's home in Peconic. Like Wigner, Teller was a first-rate nuclear physicist. Szilard had written a hopelessly complicated four-page draft of a letter to Roosevelt that he had sent ahead to Einstein to read. Together, Einstein, Teller, and Szilard decided that Szilard's original letter had to be rewritten. Szilard returned to New York and produced two new versions—a long one and a short one—and sent them to Einstein to sign. Einstein returned both letters, signed, on the 9th of August 1939. It was the longer version that eventually found its way to Roosevelt. The letter was written in English and dated August 2, 1939. It began:

> Sir;
> Some recent work by E. Fermi and L. Szilard [Fermi had also confirmed that neutrons were produced in fission], which has been communicated to me in manuscript, leads me to expect that the element uranium may be turned into

a new and important source of energy in the immediate future. Certain aspects of the situation which has arisen seem to call for watchfulness and, if necessary, quick action on the part of the Administration. I believe therefore that it is my duty to bring to your attention the following facts and recommendations:

In the course of the last four months it has been made probable—through the work of Joliot in France [Frederic Joliot-Curie was a French physicist who had married Marie Curie's daughter Irene and added her last name to his. He had also found the neutrons produced by fission, and had published this in the open scientific literature, which had driven Szilard nearly berserk.] as well as Fermi and Szilard in America—that it may become possible to set up a nuclear chain reaction [Szilard's term] in a large mass of uranium [no one yet knew how large a mass], by which vast amounts of power and large quantities of new radium-like elements would be generated. Now it appears almost certain that this could be achieved in the immediate future.

Here the letter was a little optimistic. Fermi's reactor, which was constructed at the University of Chicago using highly purified graphite to slow the neutrons released by fission, did not produce a self-sustaining chain reaction until December 2, 1942. The first nuclear explosion was set off in the desert of New Mexico on July 19, 1945. The first atomic bomb was dropped on Hiroshima, Japan, on August 6, 1945, at 8:15 A.M. An estimated 200,000 people died because of the explosion and its aftermath.

Einstein continued:

This new phenomenon would also lead to the construction of bombs, and it is conceivable—though much less certain—that extremely powerful bombs of a new type may thus be constructed. A single bomb of this type, carried by boat and exploded in a port, might well destroy the whole port together with some of the surrounding territory. However, such bombs might very well prove to be too heavy for transportation by air. [At this time, no one knew how much enriched uranium would be needed to make a bomb. It turned out that about 58 kilograms of pure ^{235}U

was enough. The fully assembled Hiroshima bomb weighed about 9,700 pounds and was readily transported by the B-29 bombers then in use.]

The United States has only very poor ores of uranium in moderate quantities. There is some good ore in Canada and the former Czechoslovakia, while the most important source of uranium is the Belgian Congo....

The letter then went on to recommend specific steps that the United States should take, including an increased funding for research on the development of nuclear energy. It concluded by noting the ominous fact that "Germany [which had just conquered Czechoslovakia] has actually stopped the sale of uranium from the Czechoslovakian mines which she has taken over." Einstein's implication, which turned out to be correct, was that the Germans had begun their own nuclear-energy program, which, at least initially, was exploring the possibility of making nuclear weapons.

Szilard added a technical memorandum reviewing all the work that had been done on fission up to that time, and he delivered the documents to Sachs in mid-August. However Sachs could not get to see Roosevelt before October 11, because in the interim the President had more pressing things to do. On September 1, the Germans invaded Poland and World War II began. When Sachs finally did get to see Roosevelt he read to him the letter that Einstein had signed. The President seemed to have his mind elsewhere.

But the next morning he had a second meeting with Sachs, and this time Roosevelt decided to create an Advisory Committee on Uranium. Szilard, Wigner, and Teller were asked to join it. Einstein was not. It does not appear that Einstein had any further contact with the nuclear program either during the war or after it. In fact the program might have died altogether had it not been for the British. In early 1940 Otto Frisch, who with his aunt Lise Meitner first understood that what Hahn and Strassmann had discovered was nuclear fission, realized quite independently of anyone else that ^{235}U could actually be used to make a bomb. By this time Frisch had emigrated to England, where he was living in the house of the distinguished theoretical physicist Rudolf Peierls, who had also emigrated to England. Together, Frisch and Peierls estimated how much ^{235}U—the so-called critical mass—would be needed to make a bomb. Much to their astonishment, their calculation gave the answer of only a pound or two. Actually they had underestimated the amount by a factor of fifty. Their result worried them deeply. A pound or two of separate purified ^{235}U did not seem like an absurd quantity to try to produce. Frisch even began some experiments on uranium purification using a method of isotope separation invented in Germany. Frisch and Peierls prepared two reports on their calculation and gave them to a physicist named Mark Oliphant, who was well placed in the British scientific establishment.

An active research program was begun under the sponsorship of the British government, and by the summer of 1941 the British had set out a plan of action to produce a bomb. This plan was communicated to the Americans in October, and it was that news, not Einstein's letter to Roosevelt, that prompted the United States to develop an atomic bomb. However, Einstein's letter made it somewhat simpler to begin such a program because the Advisory Committee on Uranium, however ineffectual, was already in place.

It is not known whether Einstein suspected that the Allies were engaged in a massive program to make a nuclear weapon from 1941 onward. He must have realized that many of the Princeton physicists had gone off to do war work. But there were many places engaged in such work. Einstein himself did some work for the navy on problems having to do with detecting submarines. When the dropping of the atomic bomb on Hiroshima was announced in August 1945, Einstein is reported to have said in German, "Oh woe." His great fear was that mankind had finally succeeded in producing an advanced and terribly destructive technological weapon without having achieved the necessary increase in political and social wisdom to deal properly with atomic energy. He immediately lent his name to various organizations that were formed to control the spread of nuclear weapons and to prevent another nuclear war.

Einstein speaks to a television audience about the great danger nuclear weapons pose to mankind. Einstein was horrified by the rapid spread of nuclear weapons and spoke out often against them.

Beginning in 1939, Einstein's younger sister Maja, along with Elsa Einstein's daughter Margot, lived with him, Elsa, and Miss Dukas at 112 Mercer Street. In 1946 Maja suffered a stroke, and she was bedridden until the time of her death in 1951. During this time Einstein would spend part of every evening in his sister's room reading to her. He read from the classics and from books such as James Frazer's *Golden Bough,* which concerns the development of thought from magic to science—a theme that would have appealed to Einstein. When the weather was good, and his health permitted, he walked home from the Institute, a distance of about two miles. Einstein was often unwell during these years. He had developed what is known as an aneurysm—an expansion of a blood vessel, caused by the weakening of the vessel's wall—in his abdomen. This is a potentially fatal condition, and Einstein was treated surgically for it. On his doctor's advice he had given up smoking his beloved pipe. During the 1950s, when the cold war with the Soviet Union was most intense, Einstein also became very concerned with the political situation in the United States. Senator Joseph McCarthy of Wisconsin had launched all sorts of wild and irresponsible investigations of scientists, and in 1954, the year before Einstein died, J. Robert Oppenheimer, then the director of the Institute for

Advanced Study and formerly the director of the United States's atomic bomb program at Los Alamos, New Mexico, lost his security clearance to work with nuclear energy. Most physicists thought that Oppenheimer had been unfairly disgraced and absurdly walled off from the military technology he had played a major role in creating. The whole atmosphere of the 1950s affected Einstein deeply, as he wrote to the queen of Belgium in 1951:

> Dear Queen:
>
> Your warm greeting pleased me no end and re-awakened happy memories. Eighteen harsh years [the period since Einstein had last seen the royal family], full of bitter disappointment have gone by since then. All the more solace and cheer are derived from those few people who have remained courageous and straightforward. It is due to these few that one does not feel oneself altogether a stranger on this earth. You are one of them.
>
> While it proved eventually possible, at an exceedingly heavy cost, to defeat the Germans, the dear Americans have vigorously assumed their place. Who shall bring them back to their senses. The German calamity of years ago repeats itself; people acquiesce without resistance and align themselves with the forces of evil. And one stands by, powerless.

In this last statement, Einstein was fortunately wrong. McCarthy was sent into disgrace and democracy continued to flourish. As a nonnative American, Einstein had been too quick to underestimate the tradition of freedom in the United States. He continued:

> Much as I should like to, it will probably not be given to me to see Brussels again. [Einstein never did return to Europe.] Because of a peculiar popularity which I have acquired, anything I do is likely to develop into a ridiculous comedy. [It is true that the news media reported anything Einstein did, from helping a child with her homework to eating an ice cream cone.] This means that I have to stay close to my home and rarely leave Princeton.
>
> I am done with fiddling. With the passage of years it has become more and more unbearable for me to listen to

my own playing. [He did continue to improvise on the piano.] I hope you have not suffered a similar fate. What has remained is the relentless work on difficult scientific problems. The fascinating magic of that work will continue to my last breath."

Einstein seemed to face the prospect of death with serenity. A few months before he died on April 18, 1955, he wrote to a friend, "And yet, to one bent by age death will come as a release; I feel this quite strongly now that I have grown old myself and have come to regard death like an old debt, at long last to be discharged." On the afternoon of Wednesday, April 13, 1955, Einstein's aneurysm ruptured. He knew that his life was in danger, but wanted nothing done to prolong it. He

Einstein in the study of his Princeton home shortly before his death on April 18, 1955.

said to his doctors, "I have done my share, it is time to go." He was moved to the hospital in Princeton, where his surviving son, Hans Albert, who had come from Berkeley, visited him. Einstein had asked for his glasses so that he could continue to work. On Sunday, April 17, he began working on an unfinished calculation that he was doing as part of the unified field theory. It was beside his bed when he died at 1:15 the next morning. As he had said to the queen, the "fascinating magic" of his work continued to his last breath.

Einstein's Legacy

When Einstein died in April 1955, a sense of loss was felt throughout the world. His name had become inextricably associated with the great issues of the 20th century—both its scientific triumphs and its tragedies, including the atomic bomb and the slaughter of his fellow European Jews. Einstein's picture had become as familiar as the picture of the members of one's own family. In a way, this is extremely odd. His work was understood by very few. Everyone knew that it was supposed to be extraordinarily difficult and that it had something to do with the atomic bomb. But if you had asked most people what relativity was, you would have drawn a blank. Even physicists—most physicists—regarded him almost as a historical monument, not someone who was relevant to the latest advances in the field. Unlike most of the other physicists of his generation, Einstein almost never went to physics conferences once he came to the United States. He gave occasional lectures at Princeton and attended a few seminars that interested him, but it is difficult to imagine him teaching a regular course or giving an invited talk at a large physics meeting.

This isolation was self-imposed. Apart from the fact that English was not his native language, something he had in common with all the European refugees who had come to this country, he seemed to think of himself as "old" almost from the time he came here. Even in the 1930s, when he was in his 60s, not old by our standards, he appeared to feel as if he belonged to another generation. This was also true of his physics. He was not very interested in the latest developments in physics. When a physicist I know tried to tell him about the new particles that were then being discovered, Einstein asked him how could one even start to understand them when one still did not understand the electron. Most physicists now feel that one can understand the electron *only* as part of a larger scheme involving the other particles.

Although Einstein invented much of what has become modern physics, he was himself really the last of the great classical physicists. His education had taken place in the 19th century. That is probably why his concerns often seem so peculiar to a contemporary physicist who accepts the quantum theory, with its probabilities and uncertainties, almost as a given. Another physicist I know wrote to Einstein with the "solution" to what he regarded as a conceptual problem in the quantum theory. Einstein wrote back that since he did not understand what the man's problem was, he did not understand his solution either. Most physicists would probably say the same thing about Einstein's concerns in the last few decades of his life. Since one did not understand what his problem was, one had a hard time trying to understand how close, or how far, he was from its solution.

Nonetheless, when we look over the landscape of contemporary physics we find Einstein's legacy everywhere, but expressed in terms that he probably would not have approved of. In recent years it has once again become "fashionable" for physicists to reexamine the foundations of the quantum theory. This process began in the early 1980s when the Irish-born physicist John Bell pointed out that

Einstein's idea of replacing the quantum theory by a more fundamental underlying construct that dispensed with probabilities and uncertainties could actually be tested in the laboratory. This work has now been done in several laboratories. Because of it, most physicists now agree that Einstein was simply wrong. If the quantum theory is eventually shown to break down, then it will not do so in any domain that appears to be accessible to our present-day laboratories. However, it may break down under extreme conditions that we can imagine and speculate about. This brings us to the subject of gravitation and cosmology, a subject that, as we have seen, in its modern form was also created by Einstein.

In 1965, Arnold Penzias and Robert Wilson, working at the Bell Telephone Laboratories, made the accidental discovery of the radiation left over from the Big Bang. This radiation is predominantly in the microwave regime—the order of centimeters in wave length—and is the kind of wave lengths used in radar. The leftover radiation is that of a blackbody with a temperature of about 2.74 degrees above absolute zero. The idea we now accept concerning its origin is that some 15 billion years ago the universe was contracted into an incredibly dense and hot state. This singular state then exploded—the Big Bang—and the universe began expanding and cooling off. The radiation produced by this explosion also cooled off until, about 300,000 years after the Big Bang, it developed its blackbody form, but at a temperature of some 10,000 degrees, as opposed to its present temperature, which has been achieved after some 15 billion years of additional cooling. What Penzias and Wilson observed were the descendants of these original photons. Incidentally, when Penzias and Wilson won the Nobel Prize for this work in 1978 they were asked by the novelist and short-story writer I. B. Singer, who had won the Nobel Prize for literature the same year, if one could actually hear the "noise" from the Big Bang. In a certain sense one can. The radiation quanta from the explosion—

about 400 in each cubic centimeter in the universe—make a hissing sound when the radio telescope that is used to observe them is connected to an audio amplifier.

As we have seen, it is Einstein's gravitational equations, modified by Friedmann, that describe the dynamics of this expansion. Though Einstein did not live long enough to learn about the "cosmic background radiation"—as the radiation fossils from the Big Bang are known—he did accept the Friedmann equations as being a good approximate description of the expanding universe. But what happens if we run these equations backwards in time? If we simply turn the crank and run the equations backwards we will arrive at an initial state that is not only extremely hot and dense but is *infinitely* hot and dense—a real singularity. Every once in a while we run into situations in physics in which the equations appear to produce singularities like this. The pre-Planck classical theory of blackbody radiation was actually an example. It predicted that a cavity full of blackbody radiation would have an *infinite* energy—something that was known as the "ultra-violet catastrophe." This result was nonsensical and was cured by the introduction of Planck's quanta. Here we seem to have an analogous situation. We appear to be in the position that if we take the Friedmann equations and run them backwards to the beginning of time we end up in a state with an infinite energy.

What are we to make of this? Most physicists believe that this means that the theory we have used to make this extrapolation cannot be pushed any further. But that theory is a mixture of general relativity and the quantum theory. To many physicists it is not surprising that this mixture has apparently gotten us into trouble. The two theories seem to come out of entirely different molds. General relativity, as Einstein formulated it, is a classical theory. There is not a word about the quantum in his papers on the subject. The theory is built on notions of space and time that a classical physicist could easily adapt to. Indeed, physicists such as Lorentz and Planck found themselves at home in it. But the quantum theory implies that these classical notions of space and time have a limited applicability. For the two theories to be compatible these limitations have to be built into the general theory of relativity, or perhaps a new theory of gravitation is needed in which these limitations are present from the start. In short, it is the very early universe that is very likely to be the "laboratory" where the quantum theory breaks down. In this laboratory gravitation is the most powerful force. In that sense it is like the center of a black hole where the usual notions of space and time give way. We are fortunate, however, to live in an epoch where new tools such as satellites and rockets continually give us new clues as to what this early universe may have been like. What is needed is a new Einstein to put these clues together into a grand synthesis. Perhaps he or she will be one of the readers of this book.

How I Did Get to See Einstein

In the fall of 1952, when I had just entered graduate school, a friend of mine was admitted to the Institute for Advanced Study as a temporary member in order to continue his research in physics. He invited me to Princeton to visit him and to see what the Institute was like. This was the first time I had been there and I was very impressed by the serene beauty of the campus. We spent a couple of hours poking around and then set off to drive to town.

We had not gotten very far when he pointed out the window. There was Einstein walking along the side of the road. You could not mistake him for anyone else. He was wearing what looked like a sailor's jacket and had on a navy blue woolen cap of the kind that seamen wear. He walked slowly but steadily. His face was creased with age. He seemed completely unaware of us, or of anyone. I wanted very much to stop the car and at least to thank him for what he had done for our science—indeed for humanity. But he was deep in thought. I don't know what about—probably his unified field theory. In any case it was the kind of reverie no one has the right to interrupt. I nodded to him. I don't know if he saw me—and we drove on.

The Michelson-Morley Experiment

In the winter of 1880-81, the American physicist Albert Michelson worked in the laboratory of the noted German physicist Hermann Helmholtz in Berlin. During that year he got the idea for his most important innovation in scientific apparatus, the so-called Michelson interferometer. To understand what this invention has got to do with relativity, we must back up a little.

Not long before Michelson's trip to Europe, the English physicist James Clerk Maxwell had taken an interest in the question of how to measure the Earth's speed through the ether. The Earth travels once around the Sun in a year, in a nearly circular orbit. Maxwell argued that there was no reason to believe that the Earth dragged the ether along with it during this orbit. It just plowed through it like a frictionless ship through the water. Hence the Earth should have a speed through the ether that is at least as great as the speed with which it orbits the Sun. This speed is easy to estimate. The distance from here to the Sun is known to be about

1.5 x 10^8 kilometers, and there are about 3 x 10^7 seconds in a year. We can use the distance from here to the Sun to compute the length of the circular orbit of the Earth. Recall that the circumference of a circle, C, is related to its radius, R, by the formula C = 2πR. Hence we can estimate the speed of the Earth, which turns out to be about 30 kilometers per second. Maxwell argued that this should also be about the speed of the Earth through the stationary ether. But how to measure it?

Maxwell had a suggestion for this. To illustrate what he had in mind, it is useful to think of the analogy of a swimmer. Suppose we have a swimmer who can swim at only one speed, call it c. Suppose this swimmer wants to swim up and back, a distance L each way, parallel to the banks of a stream. How long would the trip take? The time it takes for something to move a distance d at constant speed is always d/v, where v is the speed at which the object is moving. If the stream were not moving the answer would be 2L/c, since 2L is the total distance swum and the swimmer's speed is c. Now let us suppose that the stream is moving with a speed, or velocity, v. When the swimmer is going downstream, in the direction of the current, the combined speed of swimmer and stream is c+v. On the other hand, when the swimmer is going upstream, against the current, the combined speed of the swimmer and current is c-v. Let us call the total time for the round trip T. To find T we must add the swimmer's upstream and downstream laps:

$$T = \frac{L}{c+v} + \frac{L}{c-v}$$

With a little elementary algebra we find:

$$T = \frac{L(c-v)+L(c+v)}{(c-v)\times(c+v)} = 2\frac{L}{c} \times \frac{1}{1-v^2/c^2}$$

If the result looks strange to you, take my word that it is correct.

The important thing that I want to stress is that the

denominator in the last expression contains the ratio of the *square* of the velocity of the stream to the velocity of the swimmer. To see why this is so important, let us, following Maxwell, replace the swimmer by a light wave travelling with the speed c and the stream by the ether moving with a speed v. (We can think of the Earth as being at rest and the ether moving past it at speed v.) We can now set up a pair of mirrors separated by a distance L and ask the same question: how long will it take for the light to travel from one mirror to the other and back again? This is the same computation that we did with the swimmer, and the answer is given by the equation on the previous page. The answer depends on $(v/c)^2$. This is what Maxwell discovered. But how big is $(v/c)^2$, the ratio of the square of the speed of the earth through the ether to the square of the speed of light? I have just argued that the speed of the Earth around the sun is 30 kilometers per second, while the speed of light is about 300,000 kilometers per second. Thus the ratio v/c is about 1/10,000—one in ten thousand. But Maxwell is telling us that we must square this ratio. Doing so gives us one in a hundred million! This was Maxwell's point. He claimed that an experiment here on Earth that is sensitive enough to measure the Earth's motion through the ether would have to have an accuracy of at least *one part in a hundred million!* Maxwell was sure that such accuracies were impossible, for he did not imagine the very ingenious apparatus built by Albert Michelson.

Michelson heard about Maxwell's challenge and decided he would prove him wrong. He would devise an experiment so accurate that he would be able to measure the speed of the Earth through the ether. This is why he invented the Michelson interferometer.

The interferometer has several essential features. To the left is a source of light labeled S. In practice Michelson used a sodium flame, which burns bright yellow. This light beam is made to travel to a central point at which there is a half-

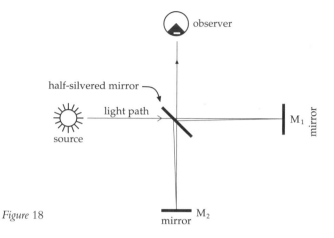

Figure 18

silvered mirror that reflects half the light beam and allows the other half to get through. As a result, the light beam is split in two. Each of the two beams produced by the split now travels along the path indicated to its respective mirror. For simplicity these path lengths are shown as being identical, although in practice they cannot be made precisely the same. This is a complication that Michelson was able to overcome with an extremely clever trick that will be described shortly. The two beams now bounce off their respective mirrors and return to the center. Because the distances over which they travel are identical, each beam takes exactly the same time to make the round-trip to its mirror and back. If the velocity of light is c and L is the length of one of the paths followed by each beam to its mirror, then the round-trip time is 2L/c. As before, the time it takes for something to move a distance d at constant speed is always d/v, where v is the speed at which the object is moving. Hence, when the beams return to the center of Michelson's interferometer, nothing interesting has happened. The high points of the light waves in one beam match up with the high points of the waves in the other beam, and the low points match up with the low points.

Remember how two waves "interfere." For example, if you drop two rocks into a pond side by side, each one will generate a circular wave. When these waves meet, they pass right through each other. But where they meet the resultant shape will in general be different from the shapes of the individual waves. This shape can be determined by "adding up" the shapes of the individual waves. That is, if a high point of one wave meets a low point of the other the resultant wave will have a reduced height at that point. But if the two wave shapes match when they meet—if every crest of one matches with every crest of the other and so on—the resultant wave will have the same shape as the individual ones. As a physicist would put it, the two waves are "in phase." The phase of a wave describes a particular point on the wave somewhere between its crest or trough.

If the two arms of Michelson's interferometer had had different lengths, the time for the round-trips of each beam would be different. The two beams would then have been out of phase when they arrived back at the center of the interferometer with their high points failing to correspond and the same being true for their low points. This would be detectable because the beams would have interfered with each other. Just like the case of the circular waves produced by the stones, this interference produces a change in shape of the wave pattern. Here, what one will see are light and dark fringes, which can be made to show up on a suitable surface. This would enable an observer to measure tiny differences in the lengths of the two arms, since the difference of path length will cause the light beams to return to the center of the apparatus at slightly different times and hence "out of phase."

How was the interferometer to be used to demonstrate the earth's motion, contrary to Maxwell's belief that it couldn't be done? Let us go back to Figure 18. If the Earth is at rest in the ether, nothing interesting happens. For simplicity I am again assuming that the path lengths of the light have exactly the same length, L. Now suppose we set the Earth in motion with a speed v. From our computation for the swimmer, we see that the round-trip time for the light that moves parallel to the direction of the Earth's motion, T, is given by

$$T= 2\frac{L}{c} \times \frac{1}{1-v^2/c^2}$$

But what about light that moves perpendicular to the direction of the Earth's motion? Here we have a somewhat different problem, involving a swimmer who wants to swim back and forth across a moving stream. A swimmer who heads directly across the stream will reach the other side at a point downstream from the swimmer's starting point since the current is moving at right angles to the swimmer. Hence, in order to hit the opposite bank at a point directly across from the starting point, the swimmer must head upstream at an angle, so that the combined motion of the swimmer and the current is just right to accomplish this. In coming back across the stream the swimmer must again head upstream in a way that is completely symmetrical to the first crossing. It is clear that this route is longer than the upstream-downstream route, and hence we expect the cross-stream route to take a longer round-trip time than the upstream-downstream route. To express this mathematically, we can focus on the speeds involved in the cross-stream trip. The swimmer can only swim at a speed c. The stream moves at a speed v. We want to know the speed at which the swimmer moves at right angles to the stream flow. Below I have drawn the relevant figure.

Figure 19

To find the velocity at which the swimmer must move at right angles to the stream we can use the Pythagorean theorem. We have

$$c^2=v^2+V^2$$

where V is the swimmer's velocity at right angles to the stream. A little elementary algebra gives:

$$V = \sqrt{c^2 - v^2} = c\sqrt{1 - v^2/c^2}$$

where I have solved for V. In this case, each lap across the stream will take a time t, calculated as

$$T = \frac{L}{c} \times \frac{1}{\sqrt{1 - v^2/c^2}}$$

Hence the swimmer's total back and forth time, T′, is twice as long:

$$T' = 2\frac{L}{c} \times \frac{1}{\sqrt{1 - v^2/c^2}}$$

Now we see that T and T′ are different, and it was precisely this difference that Michelson proposed to measure. In his experiment, the time T is the time that light takes to go back and forth in the direction of the Earth's motion, while the time T′ is the time that light takes to go back and forth at right angles to the direction of the Earth's motion. Since these times are different, the two light waves will arrive back at the center of the interferometer at different times, and their phases will not coincide. The troughs and crests of the waves will be slightly displaced with respect to each other, creating interference fringes. That is what Michelson expected to observe.

However, there is a fly in the ointment. This has to do with the fact that the two arms of the interferometer cannot possibly be designed so that they have lengths identical to each other to the one part in a hundred million accuracy we are talking about. This means that the unequal lengths will also produce interference fringes. How can one distinguish these fringes from the ones produced by the unequal times that are the consequence of the earth's motion through the ether? Here is where Michelson's brilliance came in. He floated the interferometer in a pool of mercury so that the entire apparatus could be smoothly rotated. If you rotate the apparatus by ninety degrees, the roles of the two arms are interchanged. The perpendicular arm becomes the parallel arm and vice versa. Thus, if there is a change in the effective path length, it will show up as a *change* in the interference pattern. The effects of the different lengths and the different times can thereby be disentangled.

Note that it is not necessary to take the interferometer to a special place to carry out the experiment, since *every* laboratory on earth shares the earth's motion. In fact, it would be extremely difficult to find a laboratory *not* sharing this motion, so Michelson could expect to find the displaced fringes no matter where he set up the apparatus. As it happened, he hoped to get his results in Ohio.

In 1881 Michelson joined the physics faculty of the Case School of Applied Science in Cleveland and began collaborating with a chemist named Edward W. Morley. In a five-day period in July 1887, the two men performed what is now known as the Michelson-Morley experiment. The arms of the interferometer used in this experiment were some 11 meters long. The accuracy of this device was calibrated to be one-fourth part in a billion, or more than enough to reveal the fringes produced by light traveling in parallel and perpendicular directions with respect to the earth's motion through the ether. Much to their astonishment, Michelson and Morley saw *nothing!* There was no effect. Could Copernicus have been wrong? Was the earth actually at rest in space?

Michelson was so embarrassed by this that in his Nobel Prize lecture in 1907—Michelson was the first American to win a Nobel Prize in one of the sciences—he did not even mention it, and it was not cited by the Nobel Committee as one of the reasons for giving him a prize. They apparently regarded this aspect of his work as "controversial." He simply could not accept the implications of his experiment, and to the end of his life referred to the "beloved old ether (which is now abandoned, though I personally still cling a little to it)."

At the time of the Michelson-Morley experiment, there were other physicists who also wanted to save the "beloved old ether." Among them were the Irish physicist George Francis Fitzgerald and the Dutch physicist Hendrik Antoon Lorentz—who was the physicist Einstein admired the most among all those he knew. Both Lorentz and Fitzgerald made the same suggestion. If the arm in the direction of motion would shrink by the factor

$$\sqrt{1-v^2/c^2}$$

then its shorter length would exactly compensate for the longer time of travel back and forth in the ether along the direction of motion. The problem as they now saw it was to explain how this contraction could come about. At first sight this might seem absurd. We don't see objects shrink when they move. On the other hand, we don't see objects that move at speeds near the speed of light. So we should keep an open mind. In fact Lorentz and Fitzgerald were not asking for much of a contraction, again, about one part in a hundred million. It would take an experiment with such accuracy to reveal any such shrinkage. The Lorentz–Fitzgerald contraction emerges as part of Einstein's relativity theory.

1879
March 14, 11:30 A.M. Albert Einstein born to Hermann and Pauline Koch Einstein in Ulm, Germany

1881
Einstein's sister Maria (Maja) born

1888
Einstein enters the Luitpold Gymnasium in Munich

1894
Family moves to Italy

1895
Einstein joins family in Italy; in the fall of 1895 begins high school in Aarau in Switzerland

1896
Einstein enters the ETH in Zurich; graduates in 1900

1902
Einstein becomes a patent examiner in Bern

1903
Marries Mileva Maric; first son Hans Albert born 1904

1905
The "miracle year" in which Einstein creates the foundations of modern physics.

1908
Einstein takes first teaching position at Bern.

1910
Einstein's second son Eduard born

1911
Einstein moves to Prague to teach; next year moves back to Zurich to teach at the ETH

1914
Einstein moves to Berlin; separates from Mileva

1916
Einstein publishes paper on general relativity and gravitation

1919
Einstein and Mileva divorce; general relativity is confirmed; Einstein marries his cousin Elsa

1922
Einstein wins the Nobel Prize for 1921

1932
Einstein leaves Europe, never to return

1933
Becomes a professor at the Institute for Advanced Study in Princeton, New Jersey

1936
Elsa Einstein dies

1939
Einstein signs letter to President Roosevelt warning of the dangers of nuclear energy

1940
Becomes United States citizen

1951
His sister Maja dies

1955
April 18, 1:15 A.M., Einstein dies in the Princeton Hospital

Biographies

Bernstein, Jeremy. *Einstein*. New York: Penguin, 1986.

Clark, Ronald. *Einstein: The Life and Times*. New York: Avon, 1984.

Frank, Philipp. *Einstein: His Life and Times*. New York: Da Capo, 1989.

French, A. P., ed. *Einstein: A Centenary Volume*. London: Heinemann, 1979.

Goldenstern, Joyce. *Albert Einstein: Physicist and Genius*. Springfield, N. J.: Enslow, 1995.

Ireland, Karin. *Albert Einstein*. Englewood Cliffs, N.J.: Silver Burdett, 1989.

Pais, Abraham. *Einstein Lived Here*. New York: Oxford University Press, 1994.

————. *Subtle is the Lord*. New York: Oxford University Press, 1982. The scientific parts of this book are quite difficult, but the biographical parts can be read by anyone.

Books on Einstein's Physics

Bernstein, Jeremy. *Quantum Profiles*. Princeton, N. J.: Princeton University Press, 1991.

Einstein, Albert. *Relativity*. New York: Crown, 1961.

Geroch, Robert. *General Relativity from A to B*. Chicago: University Press of Chicago, 1978.

Sartori, Leo. *Understanding Relativity: A Simplified Approach to Einstein's Theories*. Berkeley: University of California Press, 1995.

Taylor, E. F., and J. A. Wheeler. *Spacetime Physics*. New York: Freeman, 1992.

Thorne, Kip. *Black Holes and Time Warps.* New York: Norton, 1994.

Weinberg, Steven. *The First Three Minutes.* Rev. ed. New York: Basic Books, 1988.

Related Subjects

Bernstein, Jeremy. *Cranks, Quarks and the Cosmos.* New York: Basic Books, 1994.

Born, Max, ed. *The Born-Einstein Letters.* New York: Walker, 1971.

Gamow, George. *My World Line.* New York: Viking, 1970.

Manuel, Frank. *A Portrait of Isaac Newton.* Cambridge, Mass.: Harvard University Press, 1968.

AIP Emilio Segrè Visual Archives: frontispiece, 55 (Elmer Taylor), 75 (Maison Albert Schweitzer), 86 (Deutsches Museum), 124 (the Hale Observatories), 129, 133 (photo by Paul Ehrenfest), 142 (International Institute of Physics and Chemistry), 149, 165, 167; Permission granted by the Albert Einstein Archives, the Hebrew University of Jerusalem, Israel: 30, 43, 66, 105, 118; ETH Bibliothek, Zurich: 89; Historical Society of Princeton, New Jersey: 144; Library of Congress: 39, 41, 65, 101; Lick Observatory, Mary Lea Shane Archives: 113; Lotte Jacobi Archives, Photographic Services, University of New Hampshire: 16; © Stadtarchiv, Ulm: 21; original diagram by Gary Tong: 50; © Ullstein: 116, 138; U.S. Immigration and Naturalization Service: 153.

Jeremy Bernstein has been a professor of physics at the Stevens Institute of Technology since 1967 and was a staff writer for the *New Yorker* until 1993. He also serves as an adjunct professor at Rockefeller University and is a vice president of the board of trustees of the Aspen Center for Physics. He has held appointments at the Institute for Advanced Study, Brookhaven National Laboratory, CERN, Oxford, the University of Islamabad, and the Ecole Polytechnique. Dr. Bernstein has written more than 50 technical papers as well as 12 books on popular science and mountain travel, including *Albert Einstein*, which was nominated for a National Book Award, *Three Degrees Above Zero*, *In the Himalayas*, *Science Observed*, and *Cranks, Quarks, and the Cosmos*. He lives in New York City and Aspen, Colorado.

Owen Gingerich is Professor of Astronomy and of the History of Science at the Harvard-Smithsonian Center for Astrophysics in Cambridge, Massachusetts. The author of more than 400 articles and reviews, he has also written *The Great Copernicus Chase and Other Adventures in Astronomical History* and *The Eye of Heaven: Ptolemy, Copernicus, Kepler.*